G000241793

ACCLAIM F(

Creatively Malaₐⱼₐₛₑₑ

"Richards wants to shape education by story rather than by information, by resisting consumerism rather than educating for it. The goal of education, he reminds us, 'is not to make better schools, but to make a better world.' And 'the ultimate relevance of a school is what kind of civilization it inspires our children to create.' Modern industrial culture has pretty much defined education in its terms; we can do much better today and must. The metaphors, narratives and values ᴄᷤ our educational system are outmoded. A Wisdom Education Movement can bring alive new values that assure a 'nurturing, creative, joyous, inspiring place.' This book is well worth reading; and discussing; and arguing; and enacting." —Matthew Fox, author of *Creativity: Where the Divine and the Human Meet*

"Theodore Richards' book, *Creatively Maladjusted*, presents a necessary challenge and a new model to the often stale way of thinking about education. He reminds us that teachers are more than disciplinarians, and children more than robots. The creative agenda outlined in this book, along with Dr. Richards' proven experience in the field of wisdom education, are a necessity for anyone thinking seriously about education or the development of the soul: he has thoughtfully united the two and demonstıˑted why we must never attempt to separate them again. Dr. Richards has written a profound and accessible work that is as prophetic as the man behind the idea of creative maladjustment."
—Rev Julian DeShazier, Pastor and Recording Artist

—

CREATIVELY MALADJUSTED

creatively
maladjusted

The Wisdom Education
Movement Manifesto

Theodore Richards
foreword by Bill Ayers

HOMEBOUND PUBLICATIONS
Ensuring the Mainstream Isn't the Only Stream

Homebound Publications
Ensuring the mainstream isn't the only stream
WWW.HOMEBOUNDPUBLICATIONS.COM

WWW.HOMEBOUNDPUBLICATIONS.COM

Published in 2013 • Homebound Publications
Cover and Interior Design • Jason Kirkey
ISBN • 978-0-9889430-7-0
First Edition Trade Paperback

10 9 8 7 6 5 4 3 2 1

HOMEBOUND PUBLICATIONS
Ensuring the mainstream isn't the only stream.

A Dedication:

To the ancestors and to those around the world today
who have struggled and sacrificed
to give their children the greatest of gifts,
an education;

to Sue Duncan,
who taught me that education begins and
ends with compassion;

and to my mother,
my first and greatest teacher.

CONTENTS

Leaning Toward Wisdom /
Trudging Toward Freedom
foreword by Bill Ayers

Multiple Choice:

The typical American classroom has as much to offer an inquiring mind
as does:
a) a vacant lot
b) a mall
c) a street corner
d) the city dump
e) the custodian's closet
f) none of the above
(The correct answer is f—each of the others has much more to
offer an inquiring mind).

—

THE QUESTIONS THAT ANIMATE Theodore Richards' work are
the same ones I saw recently scrawled across a sprawling pan-
orama created by the tormented painter Paul Gauguin—in 1897,
after months of illness and suicidal despair, Gauguin produced on

a huge piece of jute sacking an image of unfathomable figures amid scenery that might have been the twisted groves of a tropical island or a marvelously wild Garden of Eden; worshippers and gods; cats, birds, a quiet goat; a great idol with a peaceful expression and uplifted hands; a central figure plucking fruit; a depiction of Eve not as a voluptuous innocent like some other women in Gauguin's work but as a shrunken hag with an intense eye.

Gauguin wrote the title of the work in bold on top of the image; translated into English it reads:

Where do we come from?
What are we?
Where are we going?

These questions—horrifying for Gauguin but an inspired teaching practice for Richards—rumble in the background on every page of *Creatively Maladjusted*, and they are essential for the development of a free people: Who are you? What's your story? How is it like or unlike the stories of others? How did you get here and where are you heading? What does it mean to be human in the 21st Century? How can we become more human? What qualities and dispositions and knowledge are of most value to humanity now? How can we nourish, develop, and organize full access to those valuable qualities? What kind of world could we reasonably hope to create? How might we begin?

Schools for compliance and conformity don't ask questions because they already have all the authorized and conventional answers. These places are characterized by passivity and fatalism, infused with anti-intellectualism and irrelevance. They turn on the little technologies for control and normalization—the elaborate schemes for managing the mob, the knotted system of rules and discipline, the exhaustive machinery of schedules and clocks, the laborious programs of sorting the crowd into winners and losers through testing and punishing, grading, assessing, and judging, all of it adding up to a familiar cave, an intricately constructed hierarchy where knowing and accepting one's pigeonhole on the towering and barren cliff becomes the only lesson one really needs. And this model may be perfect for a society bent on permanent war and experiencing the fatal eclipse of the public square, but it is a catastrophe for free people in a free society.

The education we've become accustomed to is neither authentically nor primarily about full human development. Why, for example, is education thought of as only kindergarten through 12th grade, or kindergarten through university? Why does education occur only early in life? Why is there a point in our lives when we no longer think we need education? Why, again, is there a hierarchy of teacher over students? Why are there grades and grade levels? Why does attendance matter? Why is punctuality valuable? Why, indeed, do we think of a productive and a service sector in our society, with education designated as a service activy? Why is education separate from production?

Theodore Richards points us toward a more vibrant and liberated space where education is linked to an iron commitment to free inquiry, investigation, open questioning, and full participation; an approach that encourages independent thought and judgment; and a base-line standard of full access and complete recognition of the humanity of each individual. He demonstrates the power of learning *from*, not *about*: from nature, not about nature, from work, not about work, from history not about history. As opposed to obedience and conformity, the work promotes initiative, courage, imagination, and creativity. In other words, the highest priority is the creation of free people geared toward enlightenment and liberation.

When the aim of education is the absorption of facts, learning becomes exclusively and exhaustively selfish, and there is no obvious social motive for learning. The measure of success is always a competitive one. People are turned against one another, and every difference becomes a potential deficit. Getting ahead of others is the primary goal in such places, and mutual assistance, which can be so natural in other human affairs, is severely restricted or banned.

On the other hand, where active work is the order of the day, helping others is not a form of charity, something that impoverishes both recipient and benefactor. Rather, a spirit of open communication, interchange, and analysis becomes commonplace. In these places there is a certain natural disorder, a certain amount of anarchy and chaos, as there is in any busy workshop. But there is a deeper discipline at work, the discipline of getting things done and learning through life.

The development of free people is the central goal of teaching toward a future free society. Teaching toward freedom and democracy is based on a *common faith in the incalculable value of every human being*, and acts on the principle that the fullest development of all is the condition for the full development of each, and, conversely, that the fullest development of each is the condition for the full development of all.

We ought to expect schools, classrooms, and education projects in a democratic society to be defined by a spirit of *cooperation, inclusion, and full participation*, places that honor diversity while building unity. These places resist the overspecialization of human activity, the separation of the intellectual from the manual, the head from the hand, and the heart from the brain, the creative and the functional. The standard is *fluidity of function*, the variation of work and capacity, the *mobilization of intelligence and creativity and initiative and work in all directions*.

On the side of a liberating and humanizing education is a *pedagogy of questioning*, an approach that opens rather than closes the process of thinking, comparing, reasoning, perspective-taking, and dialogue. It demands something upending and revolutionary from students and teachers alike: Repudiate your place in the pecking order, it urges, remove that distorted, congenial mask of compliance: *You must change!*

The importance of dialogue with one another extends to dialogue with a rich and varied past and a dynamic, unfolding future. In dialogue one speaks with the possibility of being heard, and simultaneously listens with the possibility of being changed. Dialogue is both the most hopeful and the most dangerous pedagogical practice, for in dialogue our own dogma and certainty and orthodoxy must be held in abeyance, must be subject to scrutiny.

The ethical core of teaching toward tomorrow is necessarily designed to create hope and a sense of agency and possibility in students. The big lessons are these: *history is still in-the-making*, the future unknown and unknowable, and what you do or don't do will make a difference (and of course choosing to not choose is itself a choice); *each of us is a work-in-progress*—unfinished, dynamic, in-process, on the move and on the make—swimming through the wreckage toward a distant and indistinct shore; *you don't need anyone's permission to interrogate the world*.

The schools, classrooms, and educational projects we need—and schools that we can create right now—are *lived in the present tense*. The best preparation for a meaningful future life is living a meaningful present life, and so rich experiences and powerful interactions—as opposed to school as a bitter pill—are on offer every day. A good school is *an artist's studio and a workshop for inventors*, a place where experimentation with materials and investigations in the world are an everyday happening. A good school is *fearless, risk-taking, thoughtful, activist, intimate, and deep*, a space where fundamental questions are pursued to their furthest limits.

Wisdom recognizes that the opposite of moral is indifferent, and that the opposite of aesthetic is anesthetic. The Wisdom Project creates then a range of aesthetic and ethical spaces for students to become engaged participants and not passive observers of life, and they open ground where everyone can wake up, open their eyes, and pay attention free of the blinders of ideology or habit. Students are encouraged to see it all, the splendor and the horror, to be astonished at both the loveliness of life and all the undeserved harm and pain around us, and then to release their social imaginations in order to act on behalf of what the known demands of them.

All free people deserve Wisdom Project thinking in their classrooms, schools, communities, or public spaces in order to re-ignite our democratic dreams and mobilize to change what is clearly in our hands to change. We are not allowed to sit quietly in a democracy awaiting salvation from above. We are all equal and we need to speak up and speak out about a new transformative educational practice serving the needs of a more peaceful and balanced, joyful and just community.

Knowledge is an inherently *public* good—something that can be reproduced at little or no cost, and, like love, is generative: the more you have, the better off you become; the more you give away, the more you have. Offering knowledge and wisdom to others diminishes nothing. In a flourishing democracy, knowledge would be shared without any reservation or restrictions whatsoever. This points us toward an education that could be, but is not yet, an education toward full human development—humanization—enlightenment, wisdom, and freedom.

HANDPRINTS ON THE WOMB

preface

Human salvation lies in the hands of the creatively maladjusted.
—Dr. Martin Luther King, Jr.

When my daughter was only about two years old, shortly after we had moved from California to Chicago, I used to take her on walks through the campus of my alma mater, the University of Chicago. This is not, by the way, going to be a story about exposing her young mind to the intense intellectual climate of an elite institution of higher learning. I took her there because we had been living on the grounds of a sort of urban farm in east Oakland, where a stream passed just behind our house and majestic redwoods were a short drive away, and now we lived on the south side of Chicago where there were few parks and scant places for a child to explore. The quads were green, clean, and had no cars. This was one of the few places where Cosima, my daughter, could wander. We called such excursions "adventures."

It was on one of these adventures through the quads that she taught me about education. There is a small, murky pond in one of the quads, filled with lily-pads. This seemed like a good place to stop for snack, as there were benches. But when I suggested to my daughter that she join me on a bench for snack, she would have none of it. She started poking around in the bushes, where she found a stick. She then walked over to the pond to poke the stick in the water to move the lily-pads to see beneath the surface of the water. She spent the better part of the next hour finding sticks to poke into the water.

As a parent, I had a choice that day, not unlike the choice we face now as a civilization. There was a risk in allowing her to poke around in the water. She could have fallen in, for example. If I had been on my cell-phone, texting or something, I might not have noticed and she could have drowned. Another option would have been to forbid her to play in the water. It's just too dangerous. I could have sat her on the bench and, using that same phone, done some research on ponds and told her about it. But this is not a story about the evils of technology. A book could replace cell phone in the story and changed it very little. (A book, however, seems less likely to distract one enough to not notice a drowning toddler.) This is a story about the choices we make in educating our children. And I chose another option: I let her poke her stick in the water.

The first two options—ignoring our kids as they drown or smothering them slowly with abstract information—are the choices we have made as a civilization. I will explain later where these choices have taken us. For now, it is sufficient to consider the effect they might have had on my daughter at that moment. While the effect of ignoring my daughter while she is in danger is obvious, it is less obvious why sitting her safely in a chair and lecturing her is harmful. It is a question that can only be answered by considering the principles of early childhood education.

This book is also not about early childhood education, but perhaps it should be. After all, the most important times in the development of a person are the first three years. Studies have shown that several factors contribute overwhelmingly to the development of a person in early childhood. These factors are shockingly simple.

First, we must read to our children instead of letting them watch television. A child who is read to will be far more prepared for school intellectually than one who sits in front of a television. But there is more to this argument than function. To be told a story is to enter into an experience that makes us human, one shared by every generation since we first walked out onto the African savannah millennia ago. We are at risk of losing this connection, and of losing ourselves.

Second, we must talk to our children. Language is the niche of the human. It is how we relate to our world and our capacity to communicate through language determines our survival. Nothing will contribute more to an individual's capacity for intellectual growth than language. And the younger one is, the better one is able to learn language. Anyone who has tried to learn a language as an adult can attest to this. But it is not merely talking *at* our children that matters; it is the way we speak to them. That is, we require *conversation*. Telling a two year old to sit down and shut up doesn't count as conversation.

The reason it does not count is because it is not our job to pacify a child, but to allow her to safely explore her world. If language is the tool one uses to continue to grow and learn, a spirit of exploration is the quality. We can punish our kids and TV our kids into pacification. This makes our job as parents easy, but it will make our children's lives impoverished.

So, a young child needs to safely explore her world, to share stories about her world with her elders, and to be loved. She does not need television programs that promise to make her smarter or rigid discipline that promises to make her a better person later. Rigid discipline will inhibit her capacity to think creatively, which is why most people who were disciplined harshly as children do the same to their own kids. I am quite sure every beaten child knows it is wrong—this is not because she is naïve, or stupid; on the contrary, it is because she has not yet had her capacity to think creatively beaten out of her.

But even if we are not beating our kids when they are young, even if we are talking to them—indeed, even if they are practically straight-A students who go to Harvard—we are largely doing it wrong when they get older. While most of my work has been with marginalized children, I do not believe we are doing good job with the elite, either. If we were, our elites would not be destroying our planet. There would not be such a deficit in imagination among our leaders. This is largely because of the way we educate our children. Even if an individual succeeds, our vision of success is so skewed that collectively we have still failed. The notion of allowing a two-year-old explore her world, although sadly rare, is not altogether controversial or complicated. Early childhood educators in programs like Montessori have long advocated this approach. But where is the high school equivalent? I have chosen, therefore, to write about adolescent education with the same principles in mind. The central question of this book, therefore, is this: What is the equivalent adolescent educational experience to my daughter's afternoon spent poking a stick in a pond and telling stories about it? What is the "stick" we can put it their hands and what is the "pond" in which they can poke it? Largely, we are educating our children to merely *look* at the pond, not to go beneath the surface.

—

While I love Dr. King's "I Have a Dream Speech," my favorite quote of his is this: "Human salvation lies in the hands of the creatively maladjusted." For King, salvation is not something individualistic, or entirely distinct from the world, but a process whereby we discover our selves as enmeshed in a community in which our fate cannot be separated from anyone else's. Salvation, for Dr. King, is communal. And it is not by conforming to society that we find salvation, but by transforming it.

The most radical concept in the quote is the term "creatively maladjusted." For King, like any prophet, the highest calling is not conformity to society's norms. If we are maladjusted to a corrupt system, our task is not to become "well adjusted," but to use our maladjustment as a creative, not a destructive, force.

Our school system, like pretty much any school system, serves the primary purpose of conformity. There is some value in conformity. Without some adherence to cultural norms, it would be nearly impossible to function. And cultural norms do serve positive purposes. When my daughter wants something to eat, she will often say, "I want some." As her parent, I instruct her to say, "May

I please have some?" Using this language teaches her humility, gratitude, kindness, and respect for her elders—all conservative values and values I think are worth learning. In a traditional society, learning the stories and values of a culture teaches one how to relate to one's world, one's community, and one's ecosystem. Without these values conveyed through song and story a culture disintegrates and harmonious relationship between human and nature, between individual and community, is disrupted.

But King was not talking about such values. He was specifically referring to his own struggle—called "civil rights"—in which his people were struggling for human rights in an oppressive system sustained by a culture that dehumanized them. To be maladjusted to such a system and to such a worldview was not something to be fixed; rather, maladjustment was a reasonable, moral response. Dr. King knew from his own communities and from other oppressed communities that living in such a system could make one seem mentally ill—that is, *destructive* maladjustment. He was not naïve enough to believe that all forms of maladjustment were positive. But he knew that teaching his people to try to "fit in" to a broken system was wrong and he intuited that their maladjustment could be channeled to be creative and, ultimately, transformative, salvific.

Our educational system today is as broken as Jim Crow. To succeed in such a system, one must participate in a dying culture. We put children on medication in our schools because they don't want to sit in chairs all day and learn to take tests—that is, because they are maladjusted. To understand this moment in human history is to recognize that this is not the time for blind conformity. Because all education expresses values—either explicitly or implicitly—real change in education requires challenging the values of the society we hope to transform.

—

Whether or not we begin to raise our children from birth in the manner I describe above, we can do much better with our adolescents. Just as we encourage our toddlers to explore their world, to go beneath the surface like my daughter with the stick in the pond, we can encourage our teens to explore their world, too. If we do not, even the children who had been encouraged to explore their world when they were little will only be prepared to succeed by a skewed definition of success: our scientists will know only how to exploit and destroy; our businesses will know only how to make a profit; our politicians will know only how to manipulate and oppress.

This book is not about "succeeding" in school. It is about discovering our selves, about becoming human beings in the fullest sense. It is about surviving as a species, about having more meaningful lives. The earliest human beings became human because they had the courage, the creativity, the compassion, and the imagination to venture out onto the African plains. Onto what plains must the human venture now? Will we accept this challenge, or hide behind a wall of consumerism and technology?

Some of the first art reflected the spirit of exploration that informed education for humanity until the industrial age: handprints drawn on the walls of caves. These represented how, just the child in the womb presses out at the edge of its world, we are always encountering the edge. Education, in its deepest sense, is about encountering this edge in order to discover a wisdom in ourselves. This book is about this encounter, about this wisdom, and about how we can empower our children to express their imagination. In the process, we can do better than keep them off the streets, better than encouraging them to conform to a broken system. It is my hope that, through reimagining education, our children's maladjustment can save us all.

INTRODUCTION

There seems to be near-universal agreement that there is a crisis in education today. In the United States, this tends to take the form of our failure to "compete" with the rest of the world. During the last presidential election this was a common theme; and it will be again in the next one. This dualistic vision of education as a battle in the global marketplace generally assumes that there is nothing wrong with the goals of modern education, but that we simply are not doing it well enough.

This book takes a different view. I will argue that our problem is much deeper than America's well-documented failure to compete. As the Dalai Lama says, "Education is in crisis the world over." Even those who succeed—the winners—are failing; for to succeed in the modern educational system is to lead humanity down a path of ultimate failure. We speak condescendingly of children who are "at-risk"; but what of our at-risk-civilization, -species, and -planet?

To illustrate the point, I will borrow a metaphor from the activist Van Jones, well-known to me and others in Oakland for his work for social and ecological justice there, better known nationally when he became President Obama's green jobs advocate, and still more famous when he was attacked and ultimately forced to resign from his position by the Right wing media. Originally working exclusively on issues of social justice—that is, helping the marginalized attain equal status to the elites—he eventually came to see that this approach was inadequate for the challenges of the moment, particularly the ecological crisis. We do not need to make the poor more like the rich—that will only mean that we will all fail together. We need the poor and the rich alike to radically transform our way of life. He describes his transformation as a shift in metaphor, saying he used to have the wrong metaphor, the slave-ship the *Amistad*—that is, we need to emancipate the slaves from the dungeon of the ship and bring them to the top. A more accurate metaphor, he now says, is the *Titanic*. We are all sinking together. Education is no different. Rearranging the structure of our schools is no more useful than rearranging the desks of a failing classroom—or of the deckchairs on the *Titanic*.

To figure out what is wrong with education we must first do what no one—not even educators and certainly not the politicians and bureaucrats—ever does: ask first what is wrong with our civilization. I am referring not to any particular group of people, but to global, industrial capitalism; for it is industrial capitalism, spread throughout the world by colonialism and globalization, which has defined modern education.

I will briefly identify three ways in which our species and our planet are "at-risk." First, the increasing gap between rich and poor and the marginalization of various groups of people as lead to a *crisis of injustice*. Injustice leads to wars, to violence, to terrorism. It breeds violence and suspicion. In response, we must educate our children to relate to one another in a more just and compassionate way. Second, the *ecological crisis* and mass extinction threatens to make the planet unlivable for humans. We simply cannot survive if we continue to deplete our resources and destroy the living ecosystems of the Earth. In response, we must educate our children to relate to the Earth and nature in a more integral and sustainable way. Finally, modern human beings are suffering from a *crisis of meaning*. For all the wealth some of us have amassed, our lives feel empty. We feel lost and alone. In response, we must educate our children to relate to them *selves* in more meaningful ways to live more profoundly, not just so they can acquire more money, which only feeds the three crises described above.

—

This problem begins with the way our educators are educated. Schools of education promote a utilitarianism that discourages big-picture thinking. Of course teachers need to learn the nuts and bolts of their trade; but they also need to be encouraged to think deeply about why they are teaching what they teach and why they teach it the way they teach it. As much as increased pay, treating teachers as intellectually capable will bring them the professional respect they deserve.

One could argue quite convincingly, however, that this problem is not limited to schools of education, but to all professional schools. How much perspective does one find in medical schools or nursing schools, in business or law schools? Very little, I suspect. But I would argue—recognizing that convincing counter arguments could be made—that teaching may be the most important of these professions in terms of big picture thinking. For only educators are involved with crafting the narratives upon which everyone—doctors, lawyers, and business people—will live their lives.

PROBLEMS WITH MODERN EDUCATION

One could create a long list of the problems with modern education. Most of these lists would consist of outcomes (that is, "we are failing to produce students with the following skills . . .") or professional jargon ("our schools are failing because they are using the wrong techniques or are structured inefficiently"). In both cases, it is obvious that the corporate, mechanistic, and capitalist paradigm is framing the discussion. I am not concerned with those kinds of problems because I do not believe we can properly assess either the structure or outcomes of our schools until we answer some more fundamental questions about the meaning and purpose of education. The following problems require a far more radical transformation of education than what is generally proposed in the popular discourse.

The first problem that our schools fail to address has to do with *values*. The immediate reaction of many to this statement is, "I don't want the schools to teach values; that's my job!" Others will say, "Great idea! We need to get back to good, Christian, American values." Pretty much everyone will fall into one of those two groups, which demonstrates that almost no one understands how values are actually conveyed. We do not learn are values primarily from a person talking at a group of kids and telling them what is right and wrong. That is part of it, but often—usually—we learn our values indirectly. The problem with saying that we should not teach values in schools is that we always teach values in schools, either explicitly—with the "Christian, American" values favored by conservatives—or implicitly. The implicit values taught in school today are of capitalism (we learn in order to get a good job to make money). Conservatives are right to have a problem with this, but wrong in their solution.

If we do not convey values directly, or explicitly, then how are we teaching them? Primarily, we convey values to our children through *metaphor*. Modern education teaches the wrong values because it uses the wrong metaphors. Because teachers have the wrong metaphors—and have not been taught to think deeply about them—they cannot avoid conveying certain values, even if they do not hold them.

For example, if I wanted to teach an environmentalist ethic—that is, if I personally valued the Earth and wanted to pass this on to my students—I would likely face an indifferent group of students. Surely, there would be a few students would interested in the politics of environmentalism. But my job would not be easy to begin with because most students have little relationship with the Earth, their ecosystem, or anything other than what comes to them on a screen. This challenge would be compounded by the fact that the primary metaphors at my disposal would be mechanistic rather than organic. In modern education, the living systems in which we are enmeshed and human beings themselves are understood as machines. Discussion will center on technology-based solutions that involve humans engineering solutions to the crisis. Humans are considered—in a metaphor so deep in our consciousness that we believe it to be an objective reality—to be separate from the Earth, like a mechanic working on a car. To convey to my students that they are part of an organic whole with such a metaphor is nearly impossible.

Finally, modern education makes the *wrong assumptions about how we learn*. While the two previous problems are difficult to handle given the way educators are educated, this one is more utilitarian and ought to have been better dealt with by our schools. There are many scholars who recognize the processes by which a person develops and grows. However, our schools are not populated with such scholars. And we cannot expect them to be. I would imagine that schools run by cognitive scientists would be poor schools.

But we must figure out a way to convey to our teachers how our children learn. Again, this is a problem of metaphor. Just as kids learn values by metaphor, adults can learn complex intellectual concepts through them. Teachers generally operate according to the metaphor of a student as a machine. We speak of inputs and outputs, of quantifiable results. We test our children like they are automobiles.

But our children are not automobiles, or even computers. They are as complex and chaotic as a stream. A stream can be studied and understood to an extent through quantifiable information, but not with the straightforward simplicity of a car.

ALTERNATIVES

This book is not primarily a critique of the way things are done. Although a rigorous critique of modern education is required for radical change to happen, this book is primarily a call to do something different. And while many of the criticisms and suggestions are philosophical in nature—and are indeed derived from my study of philosophy—both the critiques made and alternatives offered come from years working with youth in places like the south side of Chicago, Harlem, and Oakland. The fact that my approach to education is philosophical—that is, I am asking deep questions about what we are doing—makes it more, not less, practical, just as the fact that my educational philosophy is based on practice makes my philosophy more rigorous.

If the values of modern education are wrong, if they are part of the problem, it is because the values of Modernity are problematic. All teachers, therefore, must begin to think of their work as *subversive*. Just as Dr. King wanted his people to be "creatively maladjusted" instead of conforming to an unjust system, our students must also learn to challenge the conventions of this society. This requires teachers who can recognize this moment in human history and perceive what is at stake.

If the mechanistic and capitalist metaphors of modern education are wrong, then we require metaphors that are organic. A teacher's role is not merely to convey information, but to provide a narrative through which to understand, integrate, and give creative expression to that information. While much more can be said about metaphors that work, for now I will simply suggest that our metaphors must be organic.

Organic metaphors will not only provide a suitable narrative for our children, but also provide our educators with a way of understanding how children learn. A deeper discussion of cognitive science will come later, but for now it is sufficient to recognize that learning is not about inputs and outputs. Again, our children are not machines. Testing may be more satisfying to politicians and bureaucrats, but, in addition to the fact that it is a reflection of the wrong values, it is also less effective because it does not reflect how we learn.

Think back to the times in your life when you learned the most. Most likely, this would be a moment in which your senses were awakened, in which you were guided by passion, in which you were empowered to express your self. These are not easily-tested notions; but they represent how we truly learn. To recognize this fact—which is supported by cognitive science much more than the testing model—requires recognition of the organic nature of the human. To understand how a person learns requires an understanding of what it means to be human.

ELEMENTS OF WISDOM EDUCATION

With an understanding of these alternatives, I have laid out some of the elements of Wisdom Education. This is not intended to be the final answer. It can, and should, be an organic, evolving process that is changed and interpreted as individual teachers and students integrate it into their own experiences and express their own, unique wisdom.

The first element I will discuss is *creativity and imagination*. Largely—and increasingly—placed on the periphery of modern education, creativity and imagination play a central role in Wisdom Education for two primary reasons. First, it is through creative expression that we are able to learn concepts in a deeper way. Second, Wisdom Education recognizes that the student possesses an inherent wisdom and that, with the proper guidance, the student has something to teach us through their creative expression.

The next element is *nature*. It is difficult even to have a discussion of nature without slipping into the dualism of human-nature. Nature is a primary element of Wisdom Education because we are nature. The wisdom we possess is uniquely human, but our humanity cannot be entirely separated from nature—as it has in modern education. Nature allows our creativity to flow because it engages all of our senses. It calms us and provides us with a context for what it means to be a human being.

An educated person can think and feel, can use the left and the right brain. For our students' creativity to express a wisdom that that transformative and subversive, they must be taught the think critically. This is particularly true in a world saturated with information and media. This element, the *intellect*, is how we can train our children to discern what is meaningful information and put it in the proper context.

But education is not only about ideas. Modern education—

based largely on the mind-body dualism of Descartes—has marginalized the *body*. In Wisdom Education, our students are given practices that integrate the body into the learning process. These practices should involve both exercises for health and meditative practices to help with focus and discipline and to provide an increasingly rare time in which a young person is not at a screen, plugged in, or talking.

These practices form part of another element, *rites of passage*. Rites of passage have been part of traditional cultures until Modernity as a way to give a person a sense of place in the cosmos, to define what it means to be a human being and a participant in a culture or society. Vestiges of these rituals remain in watered-down (graduations and prom) and bastardized (gang initiation) forms. Wisdom Education recovers these rituals by providing the wisdom, nature, and body practices, and, especially, the depth, that authentic rites of passage should have.

Finally, Wisdom Education encourages our children to be *philosophers in action*. Simply put, this means that we encourage our students to ask difficult questions. The purpose of Wisdom Education, in the broadest sense, is to ask, and to begin to answer, some of these questions. Who am I? What is my place in the cosmos? What is my passion? What am I called to do at this moment in human history? Learning happens not just with asking and thinking about questions, however. We learn the most when we take ideas and put them into action.

To put all these together, we now have a vision of what it means to be a complete human being, a person who can answer the question "Who am I?" and who has the courage to go out in the world and actually do something with that knowledge. Wisdom comes forth not only through knowledge, but also through action. It is worth considering the following list, drawn from our curriculum (see Appendix A), comparing wisdom and knowledge:

- Wisdom comes forth from the ability to perceive the whole; knowledge is from a group of isolated facts
- Wisdom is perceived through the imagination; knowledge is through grasp information intellectually

- Wisdom is expressed through creativity; knowledge through information
- Wisdom requires compassion; knowledge is ethically neutral
- Wisdom and knowledge are not opposites; knowledge is required in order to be wise.

This admittedly incomplete list reveals the some of the core differences between the kind of education I am talking about and what we are currently doing in our schools.

WISDOM AS HOLISTIC
OLD AND NEW, INDIVIDUAL AND COMMUNITY

While wisdom is a complex concept that can be approached in many different ways, an important and central way to frame Wisdom Education is to describe it as holistic in contrast to the fragmentation of modern education. R. Sambuli Mosha's study of the Chagga educational system in Tanzania, *The Heartbeat of Indigenous Africa*, provides some insight in this regard. Mosha, who has been educated both in the West and in his traditional African community, explains that, for the Chagga, education is an expression of their holistic worldview. For them, the world is alive and sacred, imbued with meaning. The educational process, called *"ipvunda,"* is a process of helping a child to grow up to become a *person*, not merely to impart certain skills or facts. Values are not separated from this process. That is, to be educated, one must not only be skilled and knowledgeable, but also one must have the capacity for compassion, to know one's place in world as part of a living and interconnected cosmos.

The elders play an important role in this process. Their task is to convey to the younger generation the worldview that makes them human, that gives their lives meaning. This wisdom is conveyed in many ways, some of which are non-verbal, but a primary way that this teaching comes forth is through storytelling. Each individual story is connected to the broader narrative that tells the individual who he or she is. Storytelling, for the Chagga, is not mere entertainment, but an art, a way to connect the community to the past as they sit "around the fire" as their ancestors once did.

Always at work in the Chagga worldview is the dynamic balance between individual and community. The purpose of an education is to teach us neither to be disconnected individualists nor to eradicate our individuality. There is a subtle recognition of the paradox of individual and community. Our identity is at once unique in perspective and inextricably linked through community and ecology.

In this book, while I am drawing from traditional wisdom such as that of the Chagga, I am not suggesting that we can merely imitate either the past or a tradition of another culture. This wisdom is an important wellspring to draw on, but to apply Wisdom Education to the modern context requires something new that draws from the wisdom of the past, the wisdom of other cultures, and creates something new for the future.

THE MOVEMENT

Far more is at stake than how we run our schools. If our species is to survive the challenges of ecological collapse, of increased global instability, and of the end of the industrial age, we require an entirely new way of seeing the world, of being human. This can only be done if education is radically transformed. Modern education was created to reinforce the values that are destroying the living systems on the planet. Reforming it is simply not enough.

While this book is about ideas, it is also about practical steps toward helping to create a movement to transform education. In it, the reader will find a detailed account of the above principles and how to apply them; and the story of how I came into the movement and how you can, too. For now, the Wisdom Education movement lies on the periphery of our educational system—and perhaps this is the best place for it; for there is always wisdom at the margins. But for us to save our selves and the planet, and to allow our youth to learn and grow in more meaningful ways in order to live richer lives, we must figure out how to transform all of education.

I *A Call for Radical Change*

Education is in crisis the world over.
—The Dalai Lama

Tʜɪs ʙᴏᴏᴋ ʙᴇɢɪɴs with the claim that the way we currently educate our children is in need of a total and radical change, not mere reform. To make this case, we must first to a critical look at how we are currently educating our children. This is not intended to disparage or discredit today's educators—indeed, it is my hope that this analysis can absolve them from some of the blame that has been placed upon them. This analysis will, in fact, make it apparent that our schools do not fail due to incompetent teachers, or even poorly run schools. Our schools fail because the values upon which they are based are problematic. And these values did not originate in the school system, although they are perpetuated by it.

Before I feel comfortable laying out some of the principles of Wisdom Education, it seems appropriate to show how I came to them. This involves both a critique of the modern education system and some philosophical alternatives. But because Wisdom Education is not merely the abstract, conceptual discourse that modern education can be, I must also acknowledge my own unique perspective in the process. I begin, therefore, with my own education, the story of how I know what I know.

1

MY STORY AS A STUDENT
AND A TEACHER

M y story begins, of course, like all stories, in the womb. My development can be traced still further to my ancestors, through blood and through the ideas of those who came before me. I say this not to make an abstract philosophical point but to show that each of us does not come into the world as a blank slate; we are affected by culture and genes in complex ways. We are a process, not a collection of objects.

MY CHILDHOOD
BEHIND THE GARAGE

The best school I ever went to was behind my garage. There was no actual school behind my garage, of course, but I did learn a great deal there. I grew up in the city of Rochester, NY, in a neighborhood with ample space for a child to roam and play and in a time—the seventies and eighties—in which parents had not yet become too scared to let children roam and play. The first roaming I did was between my friend's house, directly behind mine, and the space behind our garage. It was certainly not a rural area, but

3

there were trees and bushes, cats and toads. Like many little boys, I decided to build a fort. I spent hours behind that garage, hammering away at scraps of wood, building nothing much substantial, but able to let my imagination take flight and to get my hands in the dirt. I would suggest that this phrase—"letting our imagination take flight and getting our hands in the dirt"—could be the foundational principle for the future of education.

I soon was able to venture beyond the backyard area on my own as I got older—not much older; children today would be shocked, and probably envious, at how much freedom I had at a young age. I spent my summer days riding bikes and skateboards, playing basketball and football, talking and fighting. Although I occasionally had a camp or activity to go to, I usually had no plan. I did not even have to call a friend. Just going to the local public school was usually enough to find a game to play.

As I entered adolescence, I began to wander beyond the neighborhood. I took the bus downtown with my friends, rode my skateboard to different neighborhoods, played basketball at the park. I saw a world beyond my neighborhood, and people who did not fit into its narrow socio-economic and ethnic limits. Of course, I wasted time playing video games and watching TV, and occasionally got into trouble—like most kids, I was not particularly aware of my own mortality—but I also continued to explore my world. I got my hands dirty and let my imagination fly.

At this point, the reader is probably thinking that I was some sort of urban Huckleberry Finn. So let me be clear: I was not. The other side to my early childhood education was more intellectual. I was lucky enough to come from an intellectual family—not a rich one, but one in which not only my parents but my grandparents had been to college and, in some cases, beyond. Mine was a family of preachers on one side—my paternal grandfather and great grandfather were liberal Baptist preachers—and teachers on the other. My parents spoke to me, asked me questions, and read to me. I lived in a home filled with books.

As a teacher, my mother always felt that the most important thing she could do for me was to teach me to think. She never drilled me with flashcards. Had those hideous "educational" videos existed she would not have bought them. She was annoyed by the smug parents who had taught their kids to read before kindergarten—but not to think. When I quickly surpassed them, she got to be the smug one.

Because I was well prepared for school, basic skills always came easy to me. No one ever "prepped" me for a test, but I was always well above grade level. I say this not because I want the reader to think I am a genius. I believe most children are capable of doing what I did. But the way we go about doing it is wrong. School was easy for me because I was prepared for it intellectually, because my imagination was free, and because I occasionally got my hands in the dirt.

EAST HIGH SCHOOL
MY "INNER CITY" EDUCATION

When the time came for me to go to high school, my parents could have afforded to send me to a Catholic school. Many families of our means did. The public schools were *scary*. The standards were low. But I wanted to go to East High School because East High School had one of the best basketball teams around and because, even as a young age, I had a sense of the injustice that those who had money got a better education than those who did not. Somewhat reluctantly, my parents agreed to let me go.

East was an "inner city" high school. For my European readers, some explanation is required. "Inner city" is a code word in America. Since the sixties, most American cities have been populated largely with non-white people. The closer one gets to the center of an American city, the darker the people get. While this is not precisely accurate—indeed, it is changing now—"inner city" has come to refer to non-white, especially Black and Latin American. So, while it is true that East High was not a particularly good school, it was "scary" because it was mostly Black.

I cannot claim that the academics at East were as good as those at the McQuaid, the Jesuit school my brother attended (he played football, so East had less appeal). But I learned a lot more than he did. I met people from all over the world and I began to understand injustice in America. I learned lessons that can only be taught by living. That is to say, I continued to get my hands dirty.

For example, I learned of the inequities of American society by the two-tier system of "academic apartheid" at East.[1] My honors classes often had only one or two non-White students in a school that was perhaps 20% White. Although I do not exactly recall, I probably originally assumed, like most parents, teachers, and administrators, that the students in honors classes were the most intelligent and capable. But as I got older and began—unlike most White students—to become friends with people of different backgrounds, I discovered that that many of my Black or Puerto Rican friends were smarter than the White kids in the honors classes. "Honors" classes were a way to segregate students whose parents did not want their kids in classes with too many Black kids, a means of *sorting* students by ethnicity and class.

"But what about the academics?" you ask. Yes, the academics were poor. But it made little difference. I had been prepared intellectually by my early childhood experience. I could think, I could read, and I could write. So, when I went to the University of Chicago, it took me only about a month to catch up to my peers. This is not to say that the academics at East were acceptable. They were not. It is only to demonstrate the fact that had I been given more rigorous academics—today at East, I am sure they are jumping up and down about "standards" and test scores—it would not have helped. For our adolescents, we are simply not educating for the right things.

TWO VERY DIFFERENT PLACES
THE UNIVERSITY OF CHICAGO &
THE SUE DUNCAN CHILDREN'S CENTER

The University of Chicago was a different world for me. In the beginning, I was a bit worried that I would not be able to make it.

---

[1] Jeffrey M.R. Duncan-Andrade and Ernest Morrell, *The Art of Critical Pedagogy: Possibilities for Moving from Theory to Practice in Urban Schools* (New York: Peter Lang, 2008) p.16

I had never written a real paper, had never really studied. But, as I said, I was quickly able to catch up. What seemed like it may have been an indictment of "inner city" schools turned out to be the opposite. It turned out that what really mattered were things that did not even happen in schools; it turned out that the schools that were supposed to be great—the private and suburban schools that many of my peers at the University of Chicago had attended—really did not do much that could not be learned in a short period of time. It is true that I had been better prepared than many of my high school classmates, so, of course, East High School did not provide what many students needed. But few schools do.

The University of Chicago is very good at the things it values and very poor at the things it does not. The good, for me, was my exposure to great books and fascinating ideas, and, especially, the climate of intellectual discussion and reflection. While I was there, I knew a few people who spent all their time in or around the University community (in some cases, they secretly lived in the dorm because they were dating a student) and I wonder if they didn't learn nearly as much as I did in spite of never going to class or reading a book. Of course, reading and going to class were important, but no more important than the intellectual climate.

The world I entered on the south side of Chicago was a hyper-intellectual one, ideas wielded like weapons. It is a pre-eminent example of the value-neutral space: the claim is made that only the logic of one's argument or the testability of a hypothesis determines the veracity of a concept or idea. But implicit in this worldview are values held as uncompromisingly as any fundamentalist.

Like most institutions of higher education, The University of Chicago's worldview is derived largely from ideas brought forth in and around the Enlightenment. Key to understanding this worldview is the concept of *Reason*—that it is possible to come to a conclusion about any question that is absolutely correct without regard to one's culture or personal experiences. It turns out this notion of Reason is false—according to cognitive science[2]—but it remains

---

[2] See George Lakoff, *The Political Mind: A Cognitive Scientist's Guide to your Brain and its Politics* (New York: Penguin, 2009)

embedded in our schools. Moreover, The University of Chicago's worldview is based upon a mechanical, testable universe. Absolute answers are attainable both due to the false notion of Reason and the notion that we live in a predictable, *mechanistic* world. Finally, the worldview espoused by the University of Chicago is *fragmented*. While they deserve credit for requiring students to take courses in many different subjects, students seldom integrate these divergent subjects in any meaningful way. In addition, the body and the psyche are never addressed in an academic context.

This is not to say that these values are never questioned or even subverted entirely in individual classes or by individual teachers. Frequently, they are. But they remain beneath the surface as unspoken and assumed truths. Nor is this to say that the University of Chicago is not a fine institution. I use it as an example because it is one of the best schools in the world and does Modern education as well as anyone. I am grateful to have gone there and learned a lot that was useful and meaningful. But because the school is so effective, so uncompromising, so tenacious in its Modern-ness, I also learned—although I was not yet ready to articulate it—some of the problems with Modern education.

During my third year at the University, shortly after I had quit the basketball team and was playing a pickup game at the gym, I was approached by an elderly White woman. She told me she liked the way I played and wanted to know if I was interested in working with "her children." A few days later, I came to the Sue Duncan Children's Center to see her. She hired me on the spot.

Since 1961, "Sue," as both she and her center were known to everyone, had run an after-school program on the south side of Chicago. Originally from New England, raised by Quakers, Sue worked in neighborhoods most of her peers in wealthy Hyde Park feared, long before after-school programs were popular. If you asked her why she did it, she would say, "because reading saved me, and I want to teach others so it might save them." Although she retained some of her Quaker sensibility, Sue was not a religious person in the conventional sense. Rooted squarely in the Romantic tradition—I am certain she was the only exposure most of her children had to William Blake—books and nature were her religion.

While ostensibly a tutoring program, the Children's Center was a more of a community center that was organized around books, compassion, and basketball. Unlike just about every other after school program I have encountered, Sue was less concerned with academic achievement than saving souls. She loved books because they enabled her to live a richer, more intense, more compassionate life. All around her, she saw lives impoverished not so much with lack of material things but with too much emphasis on things altogether. She loved books because they helped her—like all art—to experience the perspective of another. This compassion led her to start the center and became its ethos.

ZIMBABWE

I spent many years working for Sue. One of the benefits of working there was that she understood that her role was not merely as employer, but also as mentor and elder. Several times, she allowed me to take sabbaticals, simply because she realized I was a young man who needed to find my path and understand my place in the world. The first time I took such a leave was a year after I graduated from college. I decided to go to Zimbabwe, working for an NGO teaching women in an adult literacy program.

Although the first of a long series of currency collapses occurred the day I arrived, Zimbabwe was still a peaceful and relatively prosperous place in the 90s. In the cities, there was frustration in the eyes of the people—I could see that—but after spending a few days in Harare I was driven to a rural area in the Eastern Highlands where my work was to be done. It was a beautiful place, miles from telephones and computers; the only means of contacting the world beyond the little farm on a hill where I lived was through the mail, which arrived sporadically on the bus from the city.

My job was to teach reading, writing and arithmetic to women in various villages in the area. I was given a Zimbabwean partner, Maxwell, and we began to walk the countryside, enrolling as many participants as we could. In truth, Maxwell did most of the work. He was from the area and knew the people, the landscape, and the language. I knew a bit of Shona and even less of how to negotiate such a foreign place. The work was slow. We spent hours wandering on paths across the rugged landscape. Maxwell would ask me questions about America constantly. We became good friends.

During this time, I became exposed to the ideas of Paolo Freire, the Brazilian author of *Pedagogy of the Oppressed*. It is a complex work which I will not try to summarize here, but I can say what was most meaningful about it to me, particularly in the context of my work in Africa. Freire understood that it was not enough for elites (like me) to come to the marginalized and give them more information or skills. Authentic education, for Freire, must do something to eliminate the division between teacher and student. If I gave my students in Zimbabwe a little bit of information, but reinforced the power-relationship between us, I had done them no good.

My efforts at implementing Freire's ideas in my role in Zimbabwe were timid. I created a curriculum that I doubt was ever used. Zimbabwe, like much of the world not far removed from colonialism, had retained much of the colonial attitude in its institutions. Intelligent, creative thinkers like Maxwell worked for bosses who were best at following orders. And the Europeans who ran the NGO were far worse. They had come to Africa, it seemed to me, because they could be kings. They spoke of the Africans as if their culture had nothing to offer and that their only problem was that they had not been "developed" enough by the West—as though the West had not already done enough in Africa.

In truth, I taught my students little. These were women who had raised families on what they could grow from the parched Earth and had lived through wars. They had walked barefoot over the same land on which they were born and would never leave. Some had never been to school and were now in their eighties (this is a guess; no participant that old would know her actual age). Some did not know how to hold a pencil. What could *I* teach *them*?

But I did learn a lot. The simple experience of being immersed in a culture so different from my own—far more different than Spain, where I had spent a summer working on an archeological dig in college—taught me entirely different ways of seeing the world and challenged the assumptions and values I had held until then. I learned from the courage and tenacity of the women I taught and from the intelligence and curiosity of Maxwell. I lived in a place that was off the grid, disconnected from the internet (which I had barely used yet anyway, to be honest), telephones, and television. I learned the rhythm of the seasons in southern Africa, and learned to live according to the patterns of sun, moon, and rain—not the abstract schedules of the industrial world.

OTHER EXPERIENCES

I returned from Africa in 1998 to continue to work for Sue. I spent two more years there before taking another sabbatical, this time traveling around the world, including an overland trip across Asia. Although I was not working as a teacher, I learned a lot about myself and the world, and of course learned about education in the process.

I always devoted a great deal of time in Chicago to my study of Bagua, a Chinese martial art based upon Confucian and Taoist philosophy. Learning Bagua requires one to unlearn so many assumptions we make about the world. And unlike studying Chinese philosophy, it is an education done entirely through the body. My teacher, Tony, taught us in the basement of his apartment building. Although he was no philosopher, Tony was a true Taoist, embodying Taoist philosophy in his approach to life and his teaching. He always told us that he wanted us to become teachers more than martial artists, and had everyone—even the first time someone came to class—contribute some teaching to the class.

After returning from Asia and spending two more years working with Sue, it was time for me to move on. I was ready to do other things, to leave Chicago, and to pursue some things I was passionate about: writing, philosophy and religion. I chose schools that were the antithesis of the University of Chicago—The New Seminary in New York, Wisdom University, and The California Institute of Integral Studies in San Francisco.

In California, one of my teachers was Matthew Fox. A controversial figure, Fox had been silenced then expelled from the Catholic Church for his radical views, which included equality for women and homosexuals. More controversial than his differences with the Vatican on social issues, however, was his theology. Fox has identified a largely suppressed tradition in the West—present in other faiths and philosophical traditions as well—which he calls Creation Spirituality. Particularly threatening to the Vatican—especially the current Pope, the former Bishop Ratzinger who was largely responsible for Fox's removal—is the emphasis on the value of creation and the repudiation of the dualistic theology of Augustine. At once mystical and prophetic, intuitive and earthy, Creation Spirituality is a tradition that Fox has hoped to revive as part of a radical transformation of religion.

I met Matthew Fox at my first class at Wisdom University, formerly known as the University of Creation Spirituality (part of Naropa University)—the school he founded. After several more classes, Matt and I began to discuss his vision for transforming education and creating a program for urban youth. He met a local Hip Hop artist and filmmaker with whom he collaborated in creating the program, wrote and published a book (*The A.W.E. Project*) and began to try to find money for the project.

Two years after this process started, I received a call. Matt wanted my wife and I to become the co-directors of his pilot project.

The process of turning Matt's vision into a workable reality was not always easy. For two years, I ran Y.E.L.L.A.W.E (Youth & Elders Learning Laboratory for Ancestral Wisdom Education) in downtown Oakland. Our students came from an "alternative" high school—alternative is a euphemism for a school for students who have been kicked out of other schools, although this was not the case for all our students. Through this experience, I developed the curriculum and, along with Matt, a vision for the future of this movement. In 2009, I moved back to Chicago to start the Chicago Wisdom Project. We have been running programs for teens using the latest curriculum I created (see Appendix A). The curriculum, like this movement, like our students, and like me, continues to evolve. It is not my suggestion that the Chicago Wisdom Project or our curriculum is the final answer to the complex question that is education. It has been shaped, as I have been shaped, by my own experiences and my own unique perspective. Each version of the program can, and should, be different.

Now that I have established how I got here, I can begin to present my ideas about education. It starts by asking the question no one ever asks: Why do we have schools, anyway?

2

WHY DO WE HAVE
SCHOOLS, ANYWAY?

Many will respond to the title of this chapter by saying it is a ridiculous question. Many of those will be teachers and educators; they can be found at departments of education at fine universities and at the department of education of the federal government. Few will have even thought to ask the question and still fewer, if any, will have an answer. This, I suppose, is why they will say it is a ridiculous question.

This chapter is a discussion about the purpose of education. In order to understand its purpose, we must understand why we educate the way we do; that is, we must understand why it is that school has become synonymous with education, as though schools were the only place one could learn.

To begin, we should distinguish between *learning*, which is what education simply does in a formalized way, and *schools*. Human beings learn. More than any other species, our survival depends on the conveyance of wisdom that can be passed down, mostly through language, from one generation to the next. Ideally, this has enabled us to retain deep and intimate relationships to our surroundings and to one another.

While the importance of learning is undeniable, it is not entirely

15

a given that we should even have schools, nor should the form that schools take in the modern world be accepted without question. Here is a brief look at how and why the organic, fundamentally human process that is "learning" morphed into the formal, conscious process that is "education," and finally into the institution that is the "school."

HISTORY

It may surprise the reader that a great deal of learning happened before there were schools. Indeed, most of what we know about the world has very little to do with schools.

Learning, in the broadest sense, is required of every living being. That is to say, each species conveys information to its progeny that allows it to live in harmony with its surroundings. The capacity for harmonious relationship, for deeper connections to be made and, in the human, for more meaningful lives to be lived, is what allows for learning to become more than the conveyance of information, but also the passing on of wisdom—Wisdom Education is both a new and ancient idea. For almost the entire story of life on Earth, learning was almost entirely a genetic process. This is what we call "instinct" or the "nature" part of the nature-nurture dichotomy.

With the human, something different started to happen, something that reveals the incredible power of humanity: the capacity to convey and remember information through symbol and language. We were not the first species to learn from our surroundings or from our parents; but we were the first to develop the capacity to convey a concept through language that could be remembered and passed on. Without having to wait the millions of years it takes for genetic evolution to occur, humans could now collectively learn at a rate that accelerated exponentially.

This learning was a process of exploring the world through our urge to play, relaying our discoveries through creative expression—the myths, stories, songs, and poems that could be learned and remembered and passed down through generations—and

16

framing these discoveries in ways that allowed us to connect to our world in a meaningful way. Learning for the human, for almost all of our time in existence, was based upon wisdom, just like it had been for the oak tree and the bear and the butterfly.

Eventually, however, there were ideas and capacities that an individual must learn which parents could not necessarily teach, which required a specialist. In a traditional society, this teaching would be conveyed by an elder or shaman with a special vocation and wisdom. The purpose of this teaching was to convey to young person the mysteries of the cosmos and how the individual fits within the broader context.

Later, mystery schools arose with a similar purpose. While most education in the ancient world continued to happen at home, there was an increased interest in new forms of spirituality that required new kinds of teachers. These were the mystery schools, which set out to allow for anyone—not just the high priest or royalty—to attain individual salvation or enlightenment.

In medieval, Christian Europe—while mystery schools continued to exist on the periphery of society and Earth wisdom continued to pass on, especially among peasant women—the formal university that evolved out of the monastery represented the beginnings of the more modern, specialized type of school.[1] Although dominated by clergy, there remained the broad purpose of helping the individual find his place in the universe. Each subject was understood through the broader, Christian narrative and the medieval cosmology that informed it.

The modern school arose gradually out of the principles of the Enlightenment. There was an egalitarian ethic, particularly among the white males of the United States of America, that each individual had the right to an education. This noble sentiment had a shadow, however. The fragmentation of society was reflected in the shape

---

[1] I focus on Europe from this point on not to suggest that schools were invented by Europeans, but because I am now focusing on the Modern school, the dominant model throughout the world because of colonialism and globalization, which is causing much of the problems in education.

17

of the school. Less and less emphasis was placed on the coherence of narrative as specialization and abstraction were preferred. The emphasis on the individual in American culture and Enlightenment ideology made it far easier to draw lines between ethnicities—the concept of race was created out of this worldview—and gender. Paradoxically, the philosophy that advocated equality intensified some forms of inequality. The dominance and inequity of American capitalism cannot be removed from this picture. In spite of the dominant narrative that suggests that the public school was created to provide greater opportunities for the marginalized, part of the reason for the formation of the school was to pacify the masses. In the late 1800s, one U.S. Department of Education commissioner warned that "the children of common laborers must be educated to protect property" and to keep American industry competitive.[2]

The final shape of the school was the product of the industrial revolution. Modeled on the factory, schools shuffled students through a conveyor belt of disconnected subjects. The object was for them to get enough information to pass the test, to be a finished, marketable product. This meant, of course, that they would be ready for the factory. It is noteworthy that the factory-school has co-arisen with the factory-farm. Wendell Berry points out that the modern farm is based upon the model of a prison: "The designers of animal factories appear to have had in mind the example of concentration camps or prisons, the aim of which is to house and feed the greatest number in the smallest space at the least expense of money labor and attention."[3] Disturbingly, this is also the model for our schools. In each case, an organic process has been turned into a machine. In each case, this transformation has had disastrous consequences. There is a parallel between the cruelty to the farm animal and cruelty to the child; the processed and chemical-laden

---

[2] Walter Feinberg, *Understanding Education: Toward a Reconstruction of Educational Inquiry* (New York: Cambridge University Press, 1983) p. 87.

[3] Wendell Berry, *Bringing it to the Table: On Farming and Food* (Berkeley: Counterpoint, 2009) p.11.

food in our supermarkets and the unimaginative, chemical-laden high school graduate; and the ecological devastation perpetrated by the factory-farm and the cultural devastation of the Modern school. Indeed, we would not have factory-farms if not for a worldview shaped by factory-schools. The best students, of course, were not being prepared for the factory, but for the office. They had no better sense of their place in the cosmos, but had better test scores. They were more marketable and had better outputs. The difference between a good and bad student was not in their capacity for creativity or compassion; it was not like the difference between the bird that thrives in its adaptability and that which cannot fly well enough to survive: the difference was more like a BMW and a Pinto. The mere fact that the reader recognizes these brand names is a reflection of the degree to which the corporation has framed the modern discourse.

The educational inequalities that existed at the very inception of the American school continue to exist. I have spent much of my life working at the margins of this unjust system, and I am not the first to notice the clear connection between the bad school and the prison. For those at the bottom, they are prepared neither for the factory nor the office, but for incarceration. The punitive nature of the school, the rigidity and lack of creativity, and the segregation all prepare the youth to accept that imprisonment is consistent with the identity that has been crafted for them.

VALUES

How we educate our children is among the most profound means of expressing our values. "Educational theorists spanning the centuries from Plato to Dewey saw that the first and most important limitation on education was the values projected and manifested in the day-to-day activities of the people in the society," writes Walter Feinberg. "However important this relationship may have been in guiding the thought of educators of the past, it has been largely ig-

19

nored with the recent emphasis placed on empirical research."[4] As I stated previously, values are conveyed in education whether we do it consciously or not. I will first discuss the ways in which education can be an expression of values in a broad, historical way then refer more specifically to the values of modern education.

The brief history above put the concept of learning in the broadest possible context. Information is conveyed in most organisms through genetics. Is it possible that values are conveyed in this way? Rather than answering the question directly, I will present a couple of possible answers to the question and, after discussing the values conveyed in modern education, let the reader decide.

The first answer is that genetic evolution operates in a value-free context. Traits are passed randomly and information is conveyed unconsciously to recipients who have no choice but to embody it. The second answer does not entirely disagree with the first, but adds a layer of nuance to the discussion. While mutations are, in fact, random, the traits that are passed are not. The most uncontroversial, scientific explanation is that traits are passed that allow for the survival of a species. This could be described as a value—the survival of a species. Most of the time, this is taught in science classes as an individualistic, competitive value—each species values its own survival in isolation. But here, we have projected modern, capitalistic values—in which the value of education is the success and monetary gain it brings to each individual—onto nature. The survival of a species could also be looked at as dependent upon its capacity to have harmonious relationships to its ecosystem. That is, just as human Wisdom Education is based upon harmonious relationships, so too is the biological education that occurs through genetics.

The first form of human education was no different in terms of values, except that it was conveyed through the symbolic language of the human. Its form was poetry and song and story. But its values, at least in part, were the same—its purpose was the survival of the human, which depended upon harmony with its surroundings.

---

[4] Walter Feinberg, *Understanding Education*, p. 79.

Schools introduce another level of complexity into the discussion. Because they arise in a more complex society, there tends to be a higher degree of abstraction in a school. We learn ideas and concepts that are not necessarily directly related to our immediate survival or our immediate relationship to nature. The values of school, therefore, require a great deal more thought.

Usually, schools become a reflection of the values of a given culture. In the mystery school, the primary value is the connection of the individual to the greater, cosmic story. Later, religious schools tended to reflect specific values of particular religions—the Islamic Madrassa, for example, or the monastery.

Just as the values held by other forms of education tend to reflect that to which they owe their existence, Modern schools, arising as they did in the context of capitalism, tend to reflect the values of capitalism.

When I left Chicago and the Sue Duncan Children's Center to go to school, I tried to find work doing something other than work with children. I felt as though I was ready for something new, something that required less energy. But all my experience was working with children, so those were the only jobs I could find. Until I began my work with Matthew Fox, most of the part time work I found while in graduate school was in various after-school settings in the Bronx, Harlem, and Oakland.

Between Sue Duncan and Matthew Fox, I experienced what most youth programs are. Some of the programs were run through the Bush administration's "No Child Left Behind" program. In these programs, only that which could be quantified was valued. The only thing that mattered was the test score. The model that had failed throughout the school day was repeated after school.

Another, less-obviously problematic but perhaps more insidious value was also prevalent. Education was conflated with the attainment of money, status, and employment. When these values—basically the values of capitalism—are imposed, students are encouraged to learn to achieve a higher status in society through school, money, and employment. Students from poor neighborhoods have no incentive to contribute to their communities because leaving those communities is the goal of education. In fact, one could argue that the goal of education can be to exploit those very communities. Imagine a poor child from southern Mississippi who goes on to be an executive at British Petroleum. Would society look at him as less successful because he contributes to the destruction of his bio-region and his forefathers' way of life? Probably not.

How did we get so far away from wisdom? We cannot necessarily go back to learning as it was done in the Paleolithic Era, but we can use the natural process of learning as a foundation for learning. To uncover the values implicit in this process is not as simple as the in the Right Wing Christian school; it is a dynamic, creative process that requires new metaphors.

THE METAPHORS OF MODERN EDUCATION

Values are not generally expressed explicitly in schools. There are, of course, exceptions, particularly in conservative religious schools. But even there, a great deal of meaning is conveyed indirectly, through the metaphors that are used to shape the students' minds.

A metaphor is an individual example of broader narratives that express, perpetuate, and shape a worldview. These broader narratives are called myths. In Modernity, we have largely rejected the myth as synonymous with lie. Ironically, this is rooted in the mythology of Modernity: we have rejected this mythic form of expression in favor of the logical. This split goes back to the ancient Greeks, who used the terms *mythos* and *logos* to refer to different types of communication and of paths to the ultimate reality. *Mythos* referred to the participatory, the poetic; *logos* to the ordered and the rational. While the repression of *mythos* began with the Greeks, it accelerated in the Modern era. The mythic is now rejected to the extent that we can no longer even recognize the degree to which our own myths shape our way of seeing things. One could describe the modern myth as "the myth of no-myth."

But of course, we do have myths in Modernity as in any other culture. And while we do not sit around the fire under the stars to tell these myths (we have television commercials for that) we do convey them to our youth through the metaphors we use in our schools. I will put these metaphors in two general, interrelated categories: the mechanistic and the capitalistic.

Mechanistic metaphors begin with a basic assumption about what it means to be a human being and how the Universe operates: We are machines; the Universe operates like a machine. This metaphor operates both in terms of our overall approach to education and in terms of the way we convey ideas to our children. In the former case, we approach education as though our children were machines. We think of them as computers that require the proper input in order to have the correct outputs. This approach frames the debate around education.

A major consequence of the mechanical metaphor is the fragmentation of education. Rather than teaching our students to contextualize the information they are given as part of a coherent, interconnected whole, we teach completely separate subjects that are at best disconnected and at worst at odds. This fragmentation is no surprise considering that we think of each individual as isolated and disconnected, in competition rather than in harmony with others. The reasons for this will become apparent when considering the case of capitalism as the dominant paradigm for our schools.

Fragmentation, it should be noted, is particularly troubling in higher education, where to advance is to become increasingly disconnected from the big picture. To achieve a higher status in our society, it seems, requires that we become an expert in an increasingly obscure and de-contextualized field. The true purpose of the *univers*ity—to find one's place in the *universe*—has been lost. This is why educators are unlikely to have been exposed to the ideas I am putting forth—they were educated exclusively in education, not in being a human being.

In the latter case, we have devised curricula that reflect this assumption—that people and the world as a whole are machines, or at least machine-like—in various subjects. I had a friend who once took a job teaching high school English in the Philadelphia public schools. He chose to teach English, like many English teachers, because he loved books. After his first year, the new "CEO"—many school districts have taken to calling their leaders CEOs instead of superintendents to convey a corporate *gravitas* and capitalistic efficiency—of the public schools decided that the test scores were not high enough, so he eliminated books from the Freshman English curriculum. Let me state that again so the reader does not have to go back and re-read the previous sentence: *He removed books from the freshman English curriculum.* Instead, students were prepared for the standardized tests in a series of grammar exercises.

While I was working in Oakland for a "No-child-left-behind" program, I was given a curriculum to help my students improve their reading. Included in this curriculum were specially designed books that focused on specific skills. The books were terrible, boring to both the students and me. But exciting the students' imagination was not the issue. Books were an input; their value was based upon the immediate output, assessed through tests.

The use of technology in education is an obvious example of the mechanistic metaphor. A recent article in the Telegraph describes a U.K. proposal to replace teachers altogether with computers:

> Pupils will teach themselves in the school of the future, making teacher shortages a thing of the past, according to a "vision" outlined yesterday by the Department for Education and Skills. It said computers would transform classrooms by offering pupils "exciting new opportunities to personalize their learning." At the same time, teachers would be "liberated from their traditional role as the fount of all knowledge."[5]

This idea is neither new nor unique to the U.K. American educators, such as Diane Ravitch, the former Assistant U.S. Secretary of Education,[6] have long fixated on technology as the solution to

---

[5] http://www.telegraph.co.uk/news/uknews/1380915/Computers-to-replace-teachers.html

[6] Neil Postman, *The End of Education: Redefining the Value of School* (New York: Knopf, 1996) p. 38-39.

all our educational problems. Such an absurd notion could not exist without a mechanistic metaphor. Does no one ever think of the obvious fact that many well-educated people existed before the invention of the computer? There will be more on this subject later, but suffice it to say that such an idea completely ignores the organic, human component of education in favor an input-output based approached. That is, one can only suggest that a computer could replace a teacher if one assumes first that a human being is much like a computer—simply a less efficiently running one, encumbered by such annoyances as a body and emotions.

Because it is the field out of which technology arises, science is particularly prone to the mechanistic metaphor. As a young child, I can recall being amazed at what would fall under the category of science: I was awestruck at the stars to the point of taking classes at the planetarium; the animal world thrilled me. But after a few years of science in school, I hated it. Instead of the awe and wonder a child can experience at seeing a starry nighttime sky or encountering a wild animal, we learned lists of facts about cells to be memorized for tests.

—

The capitalistic metaphor is deeply related to the mechanistic one. Think of the way you were taught about evolution. Species "compete" against one another for survival. Like all metaphors, this is not to suggest that it is wrong. There is a certain truth to this way of thinking of the natural world, just as there is some truth to the mechanistic metaphor. Indeed, metaphors help us to understand our world when the mere facts simply cannot give us a sense of the big picture. But metaphors have consequences. When we see the natural world as a competition, it affects our relationship to it. It is much easier to plunder natural "resources" than natural "partners," much easier to kill the big bad wolf than an essential part of an ecosystem.

Just as the school debate is framed by the mechanistic metaphor, so too is it framed by capitalistic metaphors. Superintendents are

25

now "CEOs"—schools must learn the efficiency and profitability of the corporation. The latest "innovation" from Washington is a "race to the top" in which states compete for funding. The more successful a state is—success being defined through test scores—the more money they get. Such a metaphor, when carried through to its logical conclusion, virtually "guarantees failure for some," according to Jeffrey Duncan-Andrade and Ernest Morrell.[7] In a society based upon winners and losers, a society that requires some to rule and others to be consigned to menial labor, there is an unspoken and largely unconscious belief that the rich deserve more than the poor. "Perpetual urban school failure is tolerated because deep down our nation subscribes to the belief that someone has to fail in school."[8] Politicians may talk about improving our failing schools, but has any of them really ever proposed anything that would empower the youth to challenge our leaders? Why would they?

Capitalism, in the way it is framed in the popular discourse and in our schools, is related to the myth of the American Dream. The discussion about our schools, framed by this myth, centers on two interrelated concepts: the value of "rugged" independence and meritocracy. That is, each of us can become wealthy and successful (which, by the way, are pretty much the same thing in this myth) if we work hard enough, and we are personally responsible for our own success or failure. There is, of course, some truth to this myth, but it is generally not true. The exceptions to the general pattern of failure among those who were set up to fail are given as proof that we can all succeed, and success is based upon our willingness to work hard. The danger of this myth is that it subtly conveys that those who fail *deserve* to fail. School reform must therefore punish those who are failing, who happen to be the most in need of help and who happen to have already been punished the most.

Finally, capitalism defines the ultimate purpose of schools. We are in school to get a good job, to make money, and to attain a certain status. I am not suggesting that these objectives can be ignored.

---

[7] Jeffrey M.R. Duncan-Andrade and Ernest Morrell, *The Art of Critical Pedagogy*, p. 2.

[8] Ibid.

A child growing up in poverty should realize that education can be a way out of poverty and into meaningful work. But a good job does not guarantee an escape from generational cycles of under-education. In order to assure one's children of being educated, it requires not that a parent has a good job or a lot of money, but that she (the mother is usually the most important figure) develops into a life-long learner.

Moreover, the market metaphor, when applied to schools, is inaccurate. William Ayers explains:

> The market creates a class of winners and a much larger class of losers. Success in the market is realized in profit—great wealth is generated through the labor of others. The imposition of the market metaphor on a public enterprise such as schooling is filled with disingenuousness, beginning with the fact that no salable product is produced in schools, and therefore money to function must come from a public fund. The metaphor, then, is false and on its head: public money will be required, of course, but private interests will dominate the resources and benefit or profit from them.[9]

The "product" of a school is a human being, not a cell phone or an automobile. We must realize that if we are to base our schools on this metaphor, then it logically follows that we will discard the products that do not sell in the marketplace.

Metaphors operate largely on an unconscious level. A child sitting in a desk in school is as unaware of these metaphors as a fish is of water. They are simply the reality of the world. But there are alternatives.

ALTERNATIVE METAPHORS, ALTERNATIVE VALUES

The most obvious alternative to the mechanistic metaphor is the

---

[9] William Ayers, *Teaching Toward Freedom: Moral Commitment and Ethical Action in the Classroom* (Boston: Beacon Press, 2004) p. 26.

organic metaphor. This metaphor can help both the way we think about education, learning, and teaching (pedagogy) and in the specific curricular approach to various subjects. That is, we can employ the organic metaphor to help us understand the learning and teaching process as well as the subject matter itself.

Treating the learning process as organic frees us from the tyranny of testing because, while there is still some value to quantifiable outcomes, it puts test scores in the proper perspective. A test is one way of gauging how things are going for a child. I have never been one to completely dismiss a test score. (I have heard the argument many times, and I am skeptical about it, that a student did poorly on a test because he "tests poorly," as if taking a test is some mysterious skill taught by the masons or something. While I do not believe testing should be the primary way to assess a student, an extremely low test score usually indicates *something* is going wrong. I am arguing here that the test scores will actually be better in the long run if we stop fixating on them and actually start educating, which includes, we shall see later, various psychological impediments students may have to succeeding on a test.) But the actual way a child learns and what it actually means to be educated are not completely quantifiable.

To begin, the teaching and learning processes are better viewed as organic than mechanistic. This means that they are not fixed, linear processes, but complex, unpredictable ones. Learning can only arise out of dynamic relationships and meaningful experiences. The input of information and its output are therefore a small part of this process. Organic processes are inherently creative. One cannot test for specific outcomes because one cannot know what to expect.

Just as a narrative about the world has been formed out of the mechanistic metaphor, the organic metaphor gives rise to an alternative story. Because of the nature of an organic process, I cannot say exactly what this narrative will be. We must learn to trust our children with its creation. Indeed, so much of what is wrong with the way we raise our children is rooted in a lack of trust. They are micromanaged to the point that they cannot evolve or create.

A myth or narrative based upon the metaphor that each of us is deeply connected to the Universe and the natural world, that we are indeed expressions of the natural world, gives rise to values that are dramatically different from the capitalistic metaphors of the modern school. First, these values are truly universal and, at the same time, communal. The promise of rights for all of the Enlightenment has proven problematic because they are rooted in individualism and fragmentation—it teaches us that we are ultimately *separate*—which breeds competition. The organic metaphor provides us with an idea of what it means to be human that applies to all, and roots this identity in nature. We understand ourselves as fundamentally rooted in the Earth and in our communi v. Our core value based on this metaphor is compassion—we are compassionate, we feel the pain of another, because we are intimately interconnected, not ruggedly independent.

These values are not better than capitalistic ones because I like them better. They are better because they allow for a more just, more sustainable, more meaningful existence on the planet. They, or similar values, are needed if we are to survive. I would suggest that our schools, regardless of the test scores, are doing a poor job if they cannot advocate values that prevent our destruction.

SHOULD WE HAVE SCHOOLS?

With everything negative that I have said about schools, the reader may be thinking that I am proposing we abolish them altogether. I am not. But I am suggesting that we start over from the beginning, that we do not think about how to reform school, but think about how to educate a child and see what we can create. In some way, this will surely involve schools. We need places to follow our passions, to learn about the world in ways that our parents cannot teach us, and to meet different kinds of people. All these are things that a school can give us.

But if we are serious about educating our children, we must move outside the box that is a school. Schools are perhaps one of many institutions that educate a child. Moreover, we must figure out a way—and this is a largely political and bureaucratic question

29

that I cannot begin to answer—to be truly creative in the way we put together a school. Until then, the Wisdom Education movement will remain on the periphery, largely educating the youth in after-school, community-based settings. While this is not a terrible thing, it is an inescapable fact that our children spend most of their waking hours in the school, and its influence is tremendous.

3 HOW WE LEARN

CHAPTER

N ow that we have an idea about why learning and schools are important and useful, it is worth considering how one actually learns. Simply put, the discussion of the previous chapter is meaningless without understanding how human beings learn. The ideas put forth here are extensions of some of the ideas put forth in the introduction about early childhood education, as well as those of the previous chapter that put education in a broader context.

AN EVOLUTIONARY PERSPECTIVE

While I would not suggest reducing the human to our biology, it is often helpful to put education in this context. Ironically, for all the emphasis placed on the scientific method in social science that has come to dominate the discussion around education, seldom is the human placed in the broader context of its emergence through evolutionary processes. That is, we feel comfortable applying scientific methods to the statistics, technologies, and finances that dominate education, but less comfortable using it to understand the brain or placing the human in its evolutionary context. I am suggesting here

31

that evolution can be used both as a way to understand the learning process and as a metaphor for education.

As the historical overview in the previous section described, "education" begins with the genetic transfer of information. This transfer does not occur in a vacuum, however; its validity is determined by how it is expressed in the complex web of relationships that make up a community of life, or an ecosystem. The difference with human education is that we convey information through symbols, language, story, and art.

Modern educators act, however, as though the real difference is that humans learn in a void, that, unlike any other organism, we learn not to find harmony in a web of relationships but simply to convey information. Moreover, we assume that information is deposited into an empty bucket. But as William Butler Yeats reminds us, "Education is not the filling of a pail, but the lighting of a fire." Biologically, evolutionarily, and spiritually, we bring a wisdom to the world that is embedded in our very DNA. Each human being exists due to a vast history of genetic evolution, without which we could not be here. It would do no harm for our teachers to come to the classroom with this in mind.

But human education, of course, is not merely genetic, just as what it means to be human cannot be reduced to biology. We can begin the process of discovering what it means to be human—and what human education is—by looking at human evolution. Humans first evolved in Africa. To perhaps oversimplify a bit, we were apes who ventured from the forest out onto the plains. Our subsequent evolution—remember that evolution happens not in a vacuum but in relationship to one's ecology—was shaped by this venture. This, at least in the early stages of human evolution, is what makes is different from our closest relatives, the great apes who remained in the forests. A key question about our identity, therefore, is why did we leave? What was different about these adventurous apes and those who remained behind?

One possible explanation is that these apes possessed a trait called *neotony*, which is the retention of childlike traits for an unusually long time. Humans differ from all apes in the length of our childhood. And fundamental to childhood is the desire to play and explore. Carl Jung called this the "play instinct."[1] We are the apes that play and explore well beyond the first couple years of our lives. Human identity, and human learning, is shaped by our capacity and desire to play and explore. This is how we became human; for we would not have evolved as we had without it. Life on the move, on the savannah, was not easy, and it got no easier as we ventured beyond Africa. Our capacity to forge meaningful relationships in and with the new ecologies in which we found ourselves allowed us to survive. And we could not have had these relationships had we not been able to explore bravely and playfully create narratives that connected us to one another, to our predators and our prey, and to the land.

Moving forward a few million years, we have largely forgotten the value of playful exploration, particularly when it comes to adolescent education. It is as though the forest is burning to the ground, but we are the apes who tell our young not to leave the trees. In the form of tests, our schools emphasize memorization as opposed to exploration, pacification as opposed to play. The point is not that the "burning forest" that is our planet is something we must flee, but that we must, just as our ancestors did, have the imagination to relate to our world in a new way.

The concept of evolution can help us to understand education in another, metaphorical way. If we accept the fact that the forest is burning, or that the *Titanic* is sinking, where then do we find the wisdom to save our selves? Ought this not be among the primary aims of education? It would seem that reimagining our world is an educational aim consistent with the way humans have mostly learned throughout our history. Unfortunately, the institutionalization of education has made it a lumbering beast, fundamentally conservative and slow to change.

We evolved into humans not because all apes evolved into humans, but because of the actions of a few at the margins. This is

---

[1] Ken Robinson, *Out of our Minds: Learning to be Creative* (New York: Wiley, John & Sons, 2001) p. 133

how novelty emerges. There is a wisdom at the margins that those in power, because they are so immersed in the worldview that supports their power, cannot possess. "There will be some fundamental assumptions," warned the philosopher Alfred North Whitehead, "which adherents of all the variant systems within each epoch unconsciously presuppose. Such assumptions appear so obvious that people do not know what they are assuming because no other way of putting things has ever occurred to them."[2]

In contemporary education, this requires giving value to the way those at the margins of our society see the world. Because the oppressed have not benefited from society's norms, they can more easily see past them. Think of the creative explosion that has come from African-American culture, which has produced not only artistic innovation, but also new ideas and ways of seeing the world.

The youth play a particularly important role here. We could look at the necessity of schools as coming from the ignorance of youth, or we could also recognize that we can learn new ways of perceiving the world from our youth—as I believe most teachers have intuited, although it is rarely said aloud.

Wisdom, of course, just like evolution, is not all improvement on and rejection of the past. A genetic change that is too discordant with the past will not be passed on. For our youth to be able to put their creative energy to good use, they require the guidance of teachers, mentors, and elders. In my programs, I usually find having the students figure out a creative medium to express themselves fairly easy. The youth want to express themselves and want to be heard. Left to their own devices, however, the students usually would come up with something they have seen or heard on television because, the reader will recall, the television creates their narratives, and because this is what they think will impress their peers. Our youth need elders who can give them the courage to go beyond these narratives, to leave the forest behind.

---

[2] Alfred North Whitehead, *Science and the Modern World* (Free Press: New York, 1967) p.48.

WHAT DOES SCIENCE SAY?

All this may sound good, but what evidence is there that the "filling a pail" model does not work better than the "lighting a fire" one? To begin, there are few schools that light fires, so I must admit we are short on quantitative data. However, I would suggest that there are many individuals, most of them parents, who have lit fires in children. You can find some of these children at the closest Ivy School; they are those whom Paul Ray calls the "cultural creatives."[3] And while our schools continue to treat our children like pails, the quantitative data suggests that there has been little improvement in our schools over the last forty years. A University of Chicago study, for example, shows that, since peaking in the 1960s, high school graduation rates have gradually declined. Since around 1970, test scores have improved only slightly, and hardly at all when one considers the improvements of Black students after school integration.[4] That is to say that any improvements in overall achievement and graduation rates can be explained by better access for Black students, not by any efforts at reforming curriculum, methods, or even preparing students for tests. And even integration—the only significant improvement over the last forty or fifty years—has reversed in many places. Our schools are becoming no less—and in some cases, increasingly—segregated.

Most recent initiatives aimed at reforming education have claimed to be based on "scientific" methods. The U.S. Department of Education, as recently as 2002, attempted to regulate, through scripted curricula and test-centered pedagogy, teaching according what is "scientifically proven."[5] By "science" the Department of Education means outcomes that can be easily quantified through

---

[3] Paul Ray and Sherry Anderson, *Cultural Creatives: How Fifty Million People are Changing the World* (New York: Harmony Books, 2000)

[4] http://www.nytimes.com/2008/07/29/opinion/29brooks.html

[5] Kevin K. Kumashiro, *The Seduction of Common Sense: How the Right Has Framed the Debate on America's Schools* (New York: Teacher's College Press, 2008) p.47

tests. The result is a vastly narrower curriculum that focuses only on the most-easily quantified concepts. The desire for such quantification—not the desire for a more meaningful, just, or compassionate world—determines what is taught and how we teach it.

But perhaps a better scientific approach than the muddled and easily-warped business of statistics is cognitive science. Again, my aim here is not to reduce learning to science, but it would be foolish to ignore what science tells us about human cognition, particularly when the way we doing things now is supposed to be based on science. The problem is not with science, but that we have used science in the wrong way. By briefly exploring the science of the brain, I will show that the pseudo-scientific approach of Modern education, with its quantifiable this and measurable that, with its tests and goals and statistics, is completely *unscientific*. Rather, it is based on a worldview that treats the human as a machine. With this understanding, we can proceed with Wisdom Education—or, we could call it, education for humans.

The cognitive scientist George Lakoff has written extensively about how the brain works in relation to American politics.[6] His ideas apply to education as well. Lakoff is particularly critical of a mistaken notion of how people believe what they believe, the Enlightenment notion of Reason, which is disembodied, non-contextual, and non-narrative. According to the Enlightenment philosophy, our efforts at understanding something or reaching a particular belief should be based on clear and provable information—a highly difficult concept already—and a purely rational analysis ("Reason") of those facts. As it turns out, the human brain does not work this way.

The belief in Reason explains, according to Lakoff, why the Left continues to lose elections even when their policies would benefit more Americans than the Right, whose policies primarily benefit the wealthy. This is because the Left has tried to present their position in terms of facts rather than metaphors and myths, while the Right has provided people with a good story.

---

[6] George Lakoff, *The Political Mind*

Recently, for example, Barak Obama attempted to pass legislation providing health care for all. His plan would have given more people health care for less, particularly the most vulnerable of our society. But instead of arguing that this was a case of justice for the young and the poor, the latest example of America becoming more inclusive, more democratic, and more egalitarian, President Obama argued that the plan made good economic sense. He rambled on about the specific details of a complex plan. No one, including the politicians themselves, seemed to understand. In response, the Right mobilized in the form of the "Tea Party," recovering America's mythic past in the name of "freedom." In spite of the new health care legislation, the Right won the midterm elections dramatically.

When education becomes politicized, the debate over education reform is dominated by the punitive language of the Right. This includes Democrats as well as Republicans. In his campaign for mayor of Chicago, President Obama's former chief of staff, the center-left politician Rahm Emmanuel, proposed to take driver's licenses away from high school drop-outs. This ridiculous proposal was listed on his website, without a hint of irony, under the category of "Provide Students Extended Educational Opportunities."[7] While the obvious problem with the proposal is that it won't work, the more insidious problem is that it frames high school dropouts as criminals. The message is clear: students who fail are to blame and must be punished. Lakoff explains:

> Why an education bill about school testing? Once the testing frame applies not just to students but also to *schools*, then schools can, metaphorically, fail—and be punished for failing by having their allowance cut. Less funding in turn makes it harder for the schools to improve, which leads to a cycles of failure and ultimately elimination for many public schools. What replaces the public school system is a voucher system to support private schools. . . . We would wind up with a two-tier system, a good

---

[7] http://www.chicagoforrahm.com/issues/education

one for the "deserving rich" and a bad one for the "undeserving poor."[8]

The notion that our society is structured in a way to ensure the failure of a large number of students would force the elite to admit that their accomplishments are tainted, that their children are no better, no more deserving, than the children of the poor.

The Left continues to fail to understand that this is not about deception versus facts. Everyone, not just the uneducated and easily duped, believe based on metaphors and myths. It is simply how, on a physical level, the brain works. We understand the information we are given in our capacity to place it in context. There is a kind of basic, mythic structure into which all stories fit. Such a pattern is found everywhere from the core mythologies of our great cultural traditions to tabloid celebrity gossip. We respond to it physically and emotionally.

To understand a complex event—the passage of health care legislation, for example—we must put it in context. According to cognitive science, this is called a "neural binding," which links a "highly general event structure and particular kinds of actions or narratives."[9] When particular types of emotional responses are tied to particular metaphors, fitting into this mythic structure, they become connected. The Right was able to win the election because they used metaphors that elicited emotional responses and fit them into a broad, narrative structure.

This is not to suggest that the mind can be reduced to the physical brain. Too often, discussions that claim to link mind and body simply talk about each without truly connecting them. That is, what we know about the brain means that the physical, emotional, mental, and spiritual aspect of our lives are deeply interconnected. It seems obvious to me that the human is more than brain chem-

---

[8] George Lakoff, *Don't Think of an Elephant: Know Your Values and Frame the Debate* (New York: Chelsea Green, 2004) p. 32

[9] Ibid., p.27

istry, just as it is obvious that to ignore brain chemistry would be foolish, particularly when it reveals to us something profound about ourselves. The importance of the mythic way of understanding things is not merely about brain chemistry; it is an insight into how we relate to our world as participants in a great drama that is imbued with profound meaning.

Another neuroscientist, Frank R. Wilson, argues that, because the brain and the body evolved together, it is nonsensical to speak of intelligence without reference to the body. He critiques our schools for their being based upon the notion that we are filling the heads of our children without reference to the social, natural, and bodily context of the mind. Intelligence cannot be understood without reference to context and to the organism as a whole.

So what does this say about education? We do not just make political decisions based on putting information into a narrative; we understand all knowledge in this way. Presenting children with facts teaches them nothing. This is even more challenging than it sounds. In a program I was running in California, a prominent scientist and his wife came into a class to teach the kids about the amazing new insights we have about the universe. They recognized the need for metaphors and their teaching was filled with creative new ways to understand science. But although they got the metaphor part right, they failed to recognize the deeper and broader narrative that was required and the narratives the students were already working with. Some students had been raised in fundamentalists churches and thought this was heretical; others thought it was fascinating because they believed, like the scientist and his wife, in the power of science to change the world. But the majority related to the lecture as if it were another example of White people misleading them and thinking they know everything. The scientist simply could not understand where they were coming from.

But the narrative can be a teacher's ally. When I introduce something subversive or critical of the establishment to a class of marginalized youth, it is always easy to teach them. They get it because they have experienced injustice and, more importantly, their lives have been lived according to this narrative. Teachers cannot underestimate how powerful such narratives can be—they often go back generations.

All this suggests that, according to science, we must figure out creative ways to put information in the context of already-established narratives and empower our youth to recreate narratives. The youth, our teachers, and education as a whole must be a myth-making process.

HOW WE LEARN

To conclude this chapter, I will attempt to characterize how we learn from the perspective of Wisdom Education.

To begin, we should recognize that learning occurs organically and chaotically, not mechanically or predictably. What works for one person may not work for another. If, for a moment, the reader could briefly consider what he or she has learned over the years that are truly essential, things that effectively have made us who we are. Now consider exactly when and where you learned it. It is likely that you have no idea because you learned it over time as part of an organic process. And even if you do, it is likely that you learned it somewhat accidentally—perhaps some wrong turn or unexpected event. The point is that we generally do not learn the things that really matter because someone put it in a lesson plan or a curriculum. This does not mean that lesson plans and curricula are unimportant—they are—but it does mean that we should create them in order to provide an environment for learning, not to convey particular facts or skills.

This is because learning is fundamentally a process of exploration. Our job, again, is not to pacify our children, but to help to provide them with the opportunity to explore their world. If we address the question posed in the previous paragraph again, I would expect that most of us have learned most of what we consider important when we have been pursuing our passion. The task of the teacher, therefore, is to help students to discover their passion, that which gives life meaning, so they can begin to explore the world through that lens. Unfortunately, Modern education has turned this upside down: we tell our children that they can do something they want if they only put up with fifteen years or so of boredom.

If we accept the premise that having children who grow up to think critically and to challenge our world is desirable, then we must also acknowledge the wisdom they bring to the process. Of course they require guidance and discipline and structure, but we must allow ourselves to learn from the youth as well, from the wisdom at the margins. This not only empowers our youth, but also allows us to learn from them.

Finally, we learn from narrative far more than from facts. This can be understood through cognitive science, but we really do not need to dissect the brain to recognize that we understand our world primarily because of the mythology or narrative that we create. Humans have always conveyed their deepest truths through myth, expressed in stories and poems and songs and symbols. Mythology does not mean something is untrue or deceptive—it is simply the quintessentially human way of convey truths too mysterious, too deep, too paradoxical to be understood by a set of facts. Facts require context in order to become wisdom.

It is not only the passive reception of these myths that teach us, but also their expression. Creativity is central to the learning process. When we create we not only feel good—and this is, of course, an essential part of the learning process—but we also must relearn and integrate what we have been taught in a unique way. For this reason, creativity and imagination are the first of the elements of Wisdom Education.

II Elements of Wisdom Education

Education is not the filling of a pail, but the lighting of a fire.

—William Butler Yeats

T HIS SECTION WILL DESCRIBE what I consider to be the essential elements of Wisdom Education. It should not be considered exhaustive; rather, the elements described here are what I have found to be useful in my own experience. In each vision of Wisdom Education, other insights will arise that perhaps I have not thought of. Like new organisms evolving in an ecosystem, their creativity is limited only by their ability to cohere to the context of which they are part.

Wisdom Education in general, and this book in particular, is based on principles, not a preconceived notion about specific facts and skills a child should possess. I do believe that a person should have certain qualities, however, such as compassion. The six chapters in this section represent six concepts—creativity and imagination, nature, the body, the intellect, the soul, and doing—that I believe can contribute to a whole person. The current system, which concerns itself only with preparing a person to becoming a good worker/consumer and with testing for particular pieces of information, fails miserably in this regard.

While there is a curriculum in the appendix to which the reader can refer—this should be especially useful in this section—it should be viewed as only one possible way to express these principles. Moreover, it is only a half of the curriculum. The other half comes from the students, as it always does in Wisdom Education, in the form of their creative expression and imaginative insights.

4

CREATIVITY AND IMAGINATION

Perhaps no other concept distinguishes Wisdom Education from modern education so starkly as creativity and imagination. At its best, modern education marginalizes creativity and art; at its worst—which, one hopes, we have already reached—it is eliminated.

In the push to reform education in recent years, one of the strategies to bring up test scores has been to further marginalize or eliminate art programs altogether. This not only is ineffective; it also has led to an impoverished school experience for our children. When their days are spent only attempting to master prescribed a set of facts and to master a set of "useful" skills, their enjoyment of school is lost. Moreover, they create nothing, add nothing to the shared learning experience among self, peers, and teachers. And ultimately, they become less well-rounded people, but are prepared only for the office, the factory, or the prison.

A critique of the loss of art in schools can be argued in terms of outcomes. Statistics show that students who participate in some form of art—which can mean music, dance, poetry, theater . . . not just drawing and painting—do much better in school than their counterparts. In a 1995 study, the College Board—certainly a group without a bias toward the arts—showed that students who studied the arts more than four years scored forty-four points higher on math and fifty-nine points higher on the verbal portions of the SAT. This has not stopped one-third of the nation's public school music programs from being eliminated, however.[1]

But the problem is far deeper than the cutting of already-marginalized art programs. The very fact that we think of art as something peripheral, something that certain types of kids do in certain classes, speaks to the degree of marginalization that art suffers in our culture. In traditional cultures, art is something that is done by all, not only by specialists, for it is integrated into the practical functions of life. We used to sing work songs, to decorate the pottery we actually used. Because of the nature of our economy, such things are viewed as useless indulgences: Why make a pot when one can be purchased at the Walmart? Why cook dinner when we have McDonald's? Why sing a song when Brittney Spears is on the television? In school, creativity could, and should, be an integral part of every subject.

To point to the most obvious, how can we teach English without creativity? Literature is art—but few students have ever considered this fact. Instead of inspiring our children with great literature and instilling in them an appreciating of reading, we give them grammar lessons. As any writer can attest—or anyone who has been successful in school—good reading and writing happens because it is done often; and it is only done often when it is enjoyed. When a child learns to engage the imagination through reading and writing, she becomes a life-long reader. Teaching such a child to do well on a reading test requires no great skill. When a child is drilled for a reading test, the test scores may go up marginally in the short-term but the long-term prospects are dim. Such a child is a nightmare to teach—not because there is anything wrong with the child.

---

[1] Richard Louv, *The Last Child in the Woods: Saving our Children from Nature-Deficit Disorder* (Chapel Hill: Algonquin Books, 2008) p.137-138

HOW I HAVE LEARNED THROUGH CREATIVITY

I was far too old when I realized the value of being creative. As a young child, like all children, I was extremely creative. I loved to make comics, to draw, and to write. However, being far more talented at sports than "art"—which generally meant drawing—I moved away from my creative self and focused on the intellect and the body. As a young man, however, finishing up my undergraduate work at the University of Chicago, I was exposed to more ar more artists, especially in music. In part, the hyper-intellectualism of the University of Chicago turned me away from the academic and towards the creative. I was particularly drawn toward the Hip Hop movement, as I had been in high school. The problem was, for me, I was not especially talented in the media used in the realm. But I knew I had the sensibility of a poet, of an artist.

It was not until I left the United States to teach in a rural area of Zimbabwe that I began to write regularly. Each night, when I came home from my work in the field, I sat outside my door, looking out across the valleys of the Manica Highlands, and journaled. My first real effort at fiction, however, represented a sort of rite of passage. In Mozambique, which, after decades of civil war, was the poorest country on the planet, I camped in a tent next to a beach bar just outside the coastal city of Beira. It was a place in near-total destruction, so far off the beaten path that it made my Zimbabwe home—which was dozens of miles from the nearest phone—seem like a tourist trap. On my last night in Mozambique, a storm came in from the ocean, filling my little tent with water. I had nowhere to go but the bathroom. As I spent the night there, my first story (which turned into a novel) poured out. It was a story of alienation and lostness—the story that, on a profound level, had brought me there, looking for meaning. When I returned, I finally began to really write. Since then, writing has been a central aspect of my life, and each time the creative process has taught me something.

On a basic level, writing teaches us to organize thoughts and present an argument clearly. Moreover, it forces us to *have* an argument, to figure out how we feel. In creative writing—fiction and poetry—we not only figure out what we think about things, we tell stories that reveal to us who we are. My fiction and poetry has always been at least partly autobiographic. Most fiction is. Like the myth does on a macroscopic scale, it may not be exactly "how it happened," but it reveals deeper truths.

Creativity connects our inner and outer worlds. In this way, I have learned how to be authentic, to express myself without fear and self-consciousness. The shyness (and its bastard cousin, the "I'm to cool for anything" attitude) from which so many of the young suffer, is stripped away when we become true artists. For me, creativity was a way to be authentic, to be a man, in a world that did not readily offer it.

WE ARE ALL ARTISTS

If you are not particularly good at drawing, you will recall a time, perhaps in kindergarten or thereabouts, when you learned you were not a good artist. Without any malice, I suspect, some adult, perhaps a teacher, informed you of this fact. Consequently, you likely were able to discern that you were not the creative type. No need to worry, however, for you surely had figured out that being creative, while making for a nice hobby, had little to do with being a success. Much of this scenario, of course, was unspoken, or at least conveyed indirectly.

Perhaps because drawing and painting are the easiest things to teach in an art class, or maybe because they are the most easily distinguished from the emphasis on the verbal throughout the school day, art and drawing have become almost synonymous. I would like to make a distinction, therefore, between the technical skill required in any art form, and creativity. While I said above that literature is an art form, all writing, not even all good writing, is creative. A well-written newspaper article, for example, is no more creative than making cookies from a recipe provided by one's mother; and reading one requires as much imagination as eating them. Drawing is a technical skill—possessing the skill *per se* does not make one creative.

So what do creativity and imagination mean? The artistic process begins, I think, with the imagination. The imagination is an interior process—something we all possess, as human beings—of making present that which does not yet exist. It is through the imagination that we can become aware of possibilities beyond what has already happened. We make this interior process known, bring it into existence, birth it, if you will, through creativity. To be creative is to produce something knew, something that has not been considered before or at least not expressed in a particular way. Art simply adds a layer of technical proficiency—the capacity to draw or write well, for example—to this process.

It is clear that we all have an imagination. I would like to suggest that no one is any more imaginative than anyone else by birth, but that some simply have been discouraged from using their imagination or have not yet found the appropriate medium. Because we all have the capacity to, in some way, express our imagination, we are all creative. The only thing, therefore, that prevents anyone from being an artist is having some particular skill or knowledge through which to express our creativity—and, of course, the sense of awe and wonder, the feeling of inspiration, to want to express it. This ought to be considered a fundamental part of one's education. For if the skills and knowledge we are conveying to our children has truly been learned, and if it has any purpose, ought not our children be gaining the capacity to express it freshly and apply it in unique ways? Unfortunately, rather than giving a child this sense of awe and inspiration, too many children have the experience of their spirit being crushed in school.

Before explaining why this is the case, I should make one more note on the role of the artist in the modern world because it helps to explain why art and artists have been so marginalized. This goes back to the fragmentation of academia. Because we think of art as a separate and distinct category, unrelated to intellectual subjects, we have turned the artist into an oddity. And, perhaps, some kinds of art are indeed unusual. But because we have created a situation in which "art" is separate from "English," we have not only marginalized the artist; we have limited the ability of the student who is passionate about reading to be creative.

HOW WE UNDERSTAND AND TRANSFORM OUR WORLD THROUGH THE IMAGINATION

Learning involves both receptivity and productivity. Modern educators have tended to think of learning as entirely receptive; that is, they have considered learning as depositing information into an empty vessel. Freire referred to this as depositing in a bank, Yeats as filling a pail. Moreover, this receptivity is confused with passivity. It need not be. To learn, even in its receptive phase, is not an entirely passive exercise. We are not machines—"input" is not how we learn.

The receptive phase of learning requires imagination. Think of your favorite novel. Your experience of it has as much to do with the application of your own imagination to the text as with the words and ideas of the author. This is still receptive—you are not the one writing the novel—but it is not a passive receptivity.

To learn anything in a meaningful, profound way requires that we contextualize it and integrate it from our own perspective. This requires imagination. Once again, this brings us back to the basic way in which we have misunderstood the learning process. We become educated not because of how many quantifiable pieces of information we have received, but through a dynamic process of integrating information in order to express it in a unique way that transforms our world.

The creative aspect of education then allows us to relearn the information. This can be understood through the basic difference between taking a test and writing a paper. A test can demonstrate how much information one can repeat, but it cannot show the depth of one's knowledge and the wisdom of one's application of that knowledge as a paper can. A test cannot reveal the reasons behind one's answers or, most importantly, tell one's story.

To do something truly creative—an academic paper, for all its merits, is limited in this regard—not only demonstrates how well we have integrated the information. It can also help us to re-shape our world. It returns us to the primordial schools, where-in we learned through telling stories about where we have come from and our place in the world. In this way, the student becomes a teacher. Returning to your favorite novel, we must remember that its author was learning while writing, just as we now learn from their learning process. I too am learning as I write this book, just as, one hopes, you are learning from reading it. True education is not linear, but a dynamic conversation in which teachers are students and students are teachers.

CREATIVITY IN ACTION

It is impossible to place limits on the way creativity can be a part of the educational process, for to do so would inhibit the creativity of teachers and students. The first, and perhaps most important, suggestion has to do with attitude. The teacher must have an open-ness to the creativity of the student and a sensitivity to the role of the imagination in the learning process. If we think of the repeti-tion of a static fact as the culmination of education, we have closed ourselves off to the possibility that we could learn something new from our students and we have hindered the student's capacity for a profound and dynamic dialogue with the material.

The teacher, therefore, must allow the intellectual space for the student to employ the imagination. This is actually quite easy; for it has to do with doing less, not doing more. If we treat reading, for example, as an exercise in how many words can be read in a min-ute—this is actually done in schools—then we have eliminated the possibility to read with the imagination. If we never allow students to choose their own books or to play freely, we have stifled their imagination.

With adolescents, the principle remains the same. Do we have the courage to allow our teenagers to choose (within certain pa-rameters that we, as elders, mentors, teachers, and parents, set) what to do with their own time? Do we have the courage to stop giving them hours and hours of homework? Do we have the cour-

51

age to turn off the television and the video games? I would suggest that if we could actually inspire our youth and truly empower them to explore their world and express themselves, the allure of the TV would be diminished.

There are also more active, creative ways to apply this principle. I can offer a few ideas that I have used, but there are obviously many more. The process I have used has been for the majority of the creative response to come after other elements have been introduced. The idea is that we want the students to have an opportunity to integrate new ideas and new ways of looking at their world into their creative expression. Without some kind of transformation, we generally have found that the students' creativity is shaped by what they have seen on television. Young rappers want to talk about cars, money, and degrading women; young filmmakers want to re-create their favorite movie. The problems here are two-fold: first, this does not allow young people to teach anything new, to become true mythmakers for their community; and second, it simply is not particularly creative or of the quality of which our youth are capable. Our young people can do better. But there is an incredible pressure on our young people to conform. While this pressure is not entirely new, it is intensified by the degree to which they are shaped by the mass media today. Later, I will present some ideas as to how to deal with the media.

While it is important to intensify the attention given to creative expression as students have been through other elements of Wisdom Education, it is also worthwhile to allow them to express themselves to some extent from the very beginning. Even if the student is not ready to create something powerful yet—and, it should be noted, many are ready from the moment you meet them but have never been given the opportunity—creative expression can have a powerful therapeutic effect. In addition, students are usually interested in Wisdom Education primarily because of the opportunity to express them selves. Quite simply, they will get bored if they are not given some opportunity to do so early on.

The specific projects students have done are limited only by the imagination of the students, as well as practical considerations like time, money, and the expertise of the teachers and mentors available. Many of our students have used poetry as a way to express themselves without the constraints of prose. We have had students learn martial arts or work in a community garden. Older students have created workshops for younger ones.

Many students have made movies. This is surprisingly easy and cheap with the technology available today. One benefit of film is that it enables students to do collaborative projects, integrating other media such as poetry and music.

Music is always popular, especially rap. Hip Hop has been important for us for several reasons. It is a youth-centered, urban art form that integrates several media—music (rap and music production), dance (break dance), and visual arts (graffiti). Our students have done projects in each of these elements. Moreover, Hip Hop is at the center of a debate about its role in the community and has played both a redemptive, creative role and a destructive one. Some students have explored its history as a fundamentally subversive art form and its evolution as corporate interests have co-opted it.

CREATING A NEW WORLD

The ultimate role of creativity and imagination in Wisdom Education is to empower the youth to become mythmakers, to define and transform their world. This takes courage on the part of educators. We must be willing to let the youth speak for themselves. At the same time, I do not believe it is inappropriate for elders and mentors to guide the youth through this process—as long as we do so not out of a fear of something new arising, but because we know our youth can do better than repeat the same old clichés.

Creativity therefore becomes the link between every element of Wisdom Education. It is less a concept than the means by which all other concepts are linked. It is through creativity that the lines between teacher and student become blurred. And it is through creativity that the ultimate purpose of Wisdom Education is realized: We empower people to discover their place and to teach us our place in the world.

But how do we ensure that the new myths, the new stories told by our youth are the right ones for our communities? My interest in education is not only for each individual to have a more meaningful life, but also for the youth to help create a more just, more compassionate, and more sustainable future. My own daughter's possibilities, as much as they depend on me, depend on the world that the young people can help to create today. The content matters. The following element, while not a specific set of ideas or facts, will help to provide an appropriate context for this creative expression.

5

NATURE

E ast High School was a sprawling complex made up of various wings, taking up a complete city block. One small wing was referred to, quite indelicately, as "the box." I cannot say whether this was a name given to it by the students or the official one. I hope it was given by the students; for "the box" was the area of the school where special education students went. Unlike the other students in the school, they were not allowed to roam from wing to wing while changing classes. Tellingly, this is the term prisoners use to refer to solitary confinement.

Much later, it occurred to me that all schools are "boxes," based on the principle that *containment* of our youth is one of their primary purposes. Day after day, year after year, our children are put in boxes. University of Maryland professor Jane Clark calls them "containerized kids."[1] There are days, particularly in northern climes when the days grow short, when our children see no sunlight except through windows. The test scores are too low, goes the argument, so we must keep our children in school longer.

---

[1] Richard Louv, *Last Child in the Woods*, p.35

Among the great tragedies of modern life is the alienation of the human from the natural processes of which we are a part. Like most of what I discuss in this book, our alienation from nature and the Earth is not merely an educational issue; it is a problem for our species. We are destroying the planet, in part, because we have managed to delude ourselves into thinking we are separate from it. For any educational program to truly be subversive, it must challenge the dominant paradigm in the industrial world that has estranged us from the Earth.

In truth, nature is not merely a nice place to go on the weekend. We are nature. Our very existence cannot be separated from it. We could not eat, could not breath, could not survive at all without the community of life around us. To know our selves, then, is to understand the ecosystem in which we are embedded.

MY NATURE EDUCATION

While I was blessed to have grown up in a time and place in which I could get my hands dirty and explore, I did not have a great deal of exposure to nature (except of course, unbeknownst to me, that I was nature) in my childhood—more than the average child today, I suspect, but, like creativity, nature was peripheral, not at all a part of my formal education.

As a result, like most people, I thought of nature as something apart, not at all a part of my identity. As an urban child, I appreciated the culture, the diversity, the intensity of the city, but did not understand what I could learn from nature.

It was not until I was in my mid-twenties, when I went left Chicago for a training program for my work in Africa, that I realized what I had missed. Before leaving for Zimbabwe, I had to attend a training program in the Berkshires, the mountains of western Massachusetts. I spent four months there, watching summer turn to autumn and then winter. I spent hours alone in the woods, simply walking and listening.

Although I could not yet articulate it, I learned that being silent in the woods meant listening to the cosmos. Being silent in the woods allowed for a whole Universe to enter my soul. I connected to the rhythm of the seasons and the days in a way I never had before. I did not learn facts, but shifted my consciousness in myriad ways.

This transformation only intensified while I lived on the dairy farm in the eastern highlands of Zimbabwe. Each night I watched the skies come alive as the sunset faded into the starry sky. I watched the Milky Way spread out across the sky, watched the zodiac rotate, watched Orion do cartwheels. I learned to eat what could be grown and what was in season. I learned to be thankful for the rains when they came.

As the years unfolded thereafter, I sought out opportunities to commune with nature at every opportunity. I felt this need not out of any scientific, intellectual understanding for the benefits of and our relationship to nature; I understood because I had experienced a relationship—a relationship that taught me who I was.

TECHNOLOGY
A FALSE PROBLEM, A FALSE SOLUTION

It was not long ago that one heard constantly of the problem "the digital divide," the idea that poor children, especially minority children, were being left behind by their rich, white counterparts because they were not using the internet. While I would agree that this was a problem—it indeed puts one at a disadvantage not to use the internet in today's world—it was not nearly as much of a problem as it was made out to be.

Today, one hears much less of "the digital divide." My own observation has been that all kids seem to be using the internet constantly, regardless of ethnicity or class. Surprisingly, I suppose, to those who claimed that the internet would solve our educational inequities; this has not led to decreasing the educational divide. It should not be a surprise: it seems to me that pretty much the same inequalities existed before, during, and after "the digital divide."

When I have observed young people using the internet, they are not—again, many will be surprised—trying to learn about global warming or reading poetry. They are doing things like watching a street brawl on YouTube or looking at pictures of scantily-clad peers on Facebook. In fact, time spent on the internet is much like time spent in front of the television. It is something to do to turn off the mind, to disengage. The difference is that the internet does have other, more educational uses. The problem is that one has to choose to go there; and young people who have not been inspired will not. In response to a National Academy of Sciences document that claimed the internet would be an alternative for students who are "bored with the real world," Neil Postman writes, "What does it mean to say someone is bored with the real world, especially one so young? Can a journey into virtual reality cure such a problem? And if it can, will our troubled youngster want to return to the real world."[2] So the internet is a sort of Trojan Horse, brought in to our schools and after school programs to open the world up to our kids, but it ends up becoming a forum for advertising things they do not need and exposing them to more images that they cannot begin to process.

In general, I view the role of technology in education like Postman: "Like all important technologies of the past, they are Faustian bargains, giving and taking away."[3] While it is a disadvantage not to have access to certain technologies, lacking access to the internet is no more of a disadvantage than lacking access to a good library. It does not—and there is no evidence to suggest it does in spite of what many educators and politicians have suggested—provide an explanation for why certain children do poorly in school while other excel. Children who perform poorly have not been spoken to, read to, or encouraged to explore their world.

Each technology can be a sort of Trojan Horse, even if less blatantly than the internet. Plato feared that writing would lead to intellectual deficiencies if people stopped memorizing.[4] The printing press, for both good and bad, revolutionized the way humans interacted with literature. It empowered millions by giving them

---

[2] Neil Postman, *The End of Education*, p.41

[3] Ibid

[4] See Walter J. Ong, *Orality and Literacy* (New York: Taylor & Francis, 2002)

access to literature in their own tongues, but also led to a far more literal view of the world and a civilization less connected to nature and symbolic imagery. Of course we should not get rid of books. But we should look closely at what can come along with any new technology that may not be so beneficial.

A 2001 study by the Alliance for Childhood showed that thirty years of investment in computer technology had had almost no discernible benefit:

> Those who place their faith in technology to solve the problems of education should look more deeply into the needs of children. The renewal of education requires personal attention to students from good teachers and active parents, strongly supported by their communities. It requires commitment to developmentally appropriate education and attention to the full range of children's real low-tech needs — physical, emotional, and social, as well as cognitive.[5]

In fact, the study pointed out that the investment in computers—which, like the promotion of psychotropic drugs by the pharmaceutical industry, has been heavily promoted by the computer industry—has diverted funding from many other things that have proven to be beneficial.

In general, one should be cautious about technology for its tendency to discourage human interaction and the integration of the body into the learning process. Perhaps most significantly, technology-oriented learning often pushes our children to spend more time in front of screens and indoors. That is, it ignores the importance of being outside.

THE EFFECT OF BEING IN NATURE

There are also reasons that have only to do with education—that is, not with addressing the ecological crisis—for including nature

---

[5] http://drupal6.allianceforchildhood.org/fools_gold

in the learning process. Richard Louv, in his influential book *Last Child in the Woods: Saving our Children from Nature-Deficit Disorder*, documents a variety of problems that arise from a lack of time spent outside, in nature. These problems are as wide ranging as the intellectual and creative development of our children and their emotional and physical well-being.

We are better able to concentrate when we spend time in nature. Our children today are seemingly always plugged in or in front of a screen. They become accustomed to being entertained constantly with quickly-changing images—images that are designed to entice them to buy something, usually. As a result, it has become increasingly difficult to get a child to apply the kind of concentration that profound learning requires. This will be addressed further in the chapter on the body. The answer of many educators has been to give the kids more of the same, to integrate new technologies into the learning process. While some of this is appropriate—indeed, we have done it in our programs—it is not the only answer. Learning is an organic process. Screens cannot replace people; computers cannot replace nature.

When in nature, we use all our senses, whereas the television screen requires only sight and sound. A forest, for example, can be a context for the imagination to take flight. The role of nature cannot be separated from that of creativity and imagination. To be intimate with nature is to be filled with awe, to be inspired by the creativity of the natural world.

Educators seem even less aware of the need for students to get outside than they are of the importance of art in the classroom. Students who spend time in nature and are physically active will find it easier to concentrate and will have the emotional balance that learning requires. In spite of this, myriad school districts are cutting recess in favor of more time to prepare for tests. Recently, when several districts were forced to cut the school week back to four days due to budget problems, it was found that *test scores actually went up*. So much for the value of preparing for the test. In fact, several schools have shown to increase test scores through an environmentally based curriculum.[6]

[6] Louv, *Last Child in the Woods*, p. 207-208.

FOOD AS A CONNECTION TO THE WEB OF LIFE

While it can be a challenge to interest students in nature when they have spent most of their lives surrounded by concrete or being driven around from mall to mall, everyone likes food. Once an essential part of the learning process, seldom do schools integrate food into the curriculum. Traditionally, one learned in order to know what foods were safe to eat in the wild and how to procure them, to understand the rhythm of the seasons and how to grow food, and to prepare good foods. Food is not merely something that keeps us alive; it is also an expression of our culture and how we are connected to place.

The industrialization of agriculture and our subsequent estrangement from food has led to economic, ecological, and health crises in the industrial world. Understanding this process is one of the most important justice issues our children can learn about. Wendell Berry writes:

> There is, then, a politics of food that, like any politics, involves our freedom. We still (sometimes) remember that we cannot be free if our minds and voices are controlled by someone else. But we have neglected to understand that we cannot be free if our food and its sources are controlled by someone else. . . . One reason to eat responsibly is to live free.[7]

How many immigrants have come to this country in recent years due to U.S. farming policy? Why? How does this policy affect what we eat? All these are important questions to address if we are to understand the pressing issues of the day.

The best way to learn about food is to grow it ourselves. Urban farms and community gardens have become increasingly widespread in recent years. Children will be thrilled when they can eat something they have grown themselves. Creating a garden or farm teaches organizational skills. Most importantly, students begin a transformation of sense and sensibility. They begin to recognize the rhythm of the seasons and appreciate the living community

[7] Wendell Berry, "The Pleasures of Eating," 1989

61

around them. Moreover, they spend time outside, away from the boxes of classroom and television. They can get their hands dirty and let their imagination take flight, just as I used to behind my garage.

The lack of awareness around the relevance of farming to a healthy and holistic curriculum is disturbing. President Obama demonstrates in his comments about increasing the school year:

> We can no longer afford an academic calendar designed when America was a nation of farmers who needed their children at home plowing the land at the end of each day. That calendar may have once made sense, but today, it puts us at a competitive disadvantage. Our children spend over a month less in school than children in South Korea. That is no way to prepare them for a 21st-century economy.[8]

In addition to the lack of evidence that a longer school year will improve schools at all—apparently he had not heard about the rising test scores with four day weeks—the president's reasoning is flawed for a far more important reason: our estrangement from the agricultural process should not be viewed as an inevitable sign of irreversible progress, but as a crisis. While I understand his desire, and the desire of educators from whom the president takes his cues on this issue, to deal with the problem that our children spend their summers and after-school time watching television, our task as educators must be to find better ways for our children to spend their free time, not eradicate the notion of free time altogether. Maybe we should consider that our young people *should* be plowing the land, not locked away in a classroom. The values expressed in this quote are telling. The purpose of education, according to the president, is to prepare our youth for "the 21st century economy." The typical values of utilitarianism and capitalism—the assumption that education is "competitive"—rise to the fore. The irony is that

[8] http://seattletimes.nwsource.com/html/politics/2008838703_schools11.html

I am fairly certain that the president was not educated in this way. If one were to ask him how he became the man he is today—and while I am criticizing him on this matter, I think he has many admirable qualities—he would surely not point to being prepared for the 21ˢᵗ century economy. And I doubt he educates his own children with this in mind.

This is one among many examples of how, although clearly more committed to education than the Republicans, the philosophy of the two parties remains fundamentally the same. While Democrats are quite right to criticize George W. Bush for the No Child Left Behind debacle, it should be remembered that they usually do so only because of the Republicans failure to fund the bill—not because of its focus on testing, with which they basically agree, or at least can offer no alternative.

The lessons of farming truly coming alive for the youth when they begin to harvest, prepare, and eat what they have grown. Cooking is a hands-on way for students to learn myriad lessons, seeing their profound connection to the living world through their food.

It is hardly controversial to suggest that there is an epidemic health crisis among our children due to their diets. The rate of type 2 diabetes in children, once only found in adults, is soaring, particularly among Black and Hispanic children. Obesity has never been greater. Our leaders take away free-time and eliminate recess, limit the time a parent can be home with children to prepare food, and wonder why these problems are on the rise. Criticizing the victims—blaming obese children for lacking discipline—is the common response.

By growing, cooking, and eating their food, the youth can see an alternative to fast food and chips. They can learn the skills, knowledge, and creativity required to garden and cook. Moreover, they can begin to recognize the relationship between the obesity of the American child and the malnourishment of children in the global South by exploring the industrial food system that is so different from the simple and beautiful process of growing and preparing one's own vegetables and fruits.

If one's garden is big enough, the youth can learn to can and store, as well as sell, their produce. While I have criticized the values of *global industrial* capitalism, I see nothing wrong with starting a small business with young people. In fact, it can teach many lessons, both practical and academic.

The culmination of these lessons on food, of course, is eating. This will surely not be lost on any group of kids. We do not share food as much as we used to. This impoverishes us spiritually and diminishes our sense of community. To share food is essential to our humanity. Any teacher, in any type of classroom, will find his job much easier if students are preparing and sharing food together. While most schools, I suspect, will say that this is too costly and takes too much time that could be spent on learning basic skills for tests, a deeper analysis suggests otherwise. How much money is wasted on drugs for children who cannot concentrate because they have too much sugar in their diets? There have been documented cases of children dramatically changing their behavior as their diets have changed. Moreover, sharing meals brings about a spirit of community in a classroom or youth group. We learn in community, from one another, and food can be a catalyst for this process.

EVOLUTION
WE ARE NATURE

We are nature. Any discussion about nature is extraordinarily difficult because of the tendency to reinforce the dualism of the human and nature. Nature is not place to visit; it is that from which we arise. The human body is nature. We have evolved not only *from* the Earth, but also *within* the Earth. The point is that, when we truly understand how we have evolved, the lines between the human and nature become blurred. Our identity, so fundamental to the basic purpose of education, cannot be isolated in the mind, walled in behind our skulls.

In any science curriculum, evolution is a core concept, *the* core concept around which the study of biology is organized. This is significant not merely because it is an interesting theory about science; its significance lies in what it tells us about ourselves. Evolution tells us who we are.

We cannot teach our youth a particular narrative in science without having the courage—and I say courage because there will be fundamentalists who understand neither the Bible nor evolution who will make this politically difficult—the courage to integrate it into the students' pursuit of understanding themselves and their world. It does not mean telling them what evolution should make them believe. Rather, it means showing them the evide ce for evolution and challenging them to develop a narrative that is both personally meaningful and intellectually rigorous.

THE STORY OF THE UNIVERSE,
THE STORY OF OUR SELVES

Wisdom Education has always been about answering fundamental questions such as "Who am I?" Until the modern period, much of this understanding came from a myth, a narrative or story that described how we came into being. The creation myth made sense of our world and our place in it while showing how we were at once connected and unique. In a tı..ditional or indigenous society, there were no academic "subjects"—everything was understood through the lens of the myth. And even when subjects did arise—in a medieval school, for example—they were still understood through a common lens. We can now criticize the lens—I am not advocating basing a curriculum on Scholastic theology—but we have to find a new lens to replace it.

What, then, is the lens through which we can organize a new Wisdom curriculum? One possibility is by looking at the world in terms of ancestry, which is essentially what the creation myth of an indigenous society does. The difference, however, is that ours is a pluralistic society that derives much of its knowledge about the world through science.

Modern, industrial society is marked by an abundance of information, uncovered by science and made available through technology. The problem is that the diversity of our society and the overwhelming amount of information make it difficult to find a coherent narrative around which to organize a curriculum. I would suggest that nature itself as understood by modern science can provide the foundation of just such a narrative, a narrative that can be both pluralistic and unifying.

I am not suggesting that we introduce any more information into a school curriculum than what is pretty much already there. The information that scientists completely agree on about the Universe goes something like this:

The story of the Universe is the story of each of us. Each phase, each moment in this story is the Universe giving birth to us. Each moment represents the birth of our common ancestor. As the process unfolds, there is a paradox of differentiation/subjectivity or interiority/communion that unfolds as well. The Universe becomes more differentiated as it gives rise to the capacity of individuals—like us—to experience a deeper interior life and to connect to others.

Out of unimaginable light the universe was dreamed into being. It contained all the light, energy, and potential for everything that would ever come to be, all contained within the vessel of hydrogen. 13.7 Billion years ago, the primordial fireball gave birth to the Universe. In the fecund quantum vacuum, space exists, but not time.

13.3 Billion years ago, the first stars were born.

12.7 Billion years ago, the first galaxies. These stars possess only hydrogen and helium, but have the capacity to produce the elements that make life possible. The galaxies recreate stars with these new elements.

7 Billion years ago. Dark energy overpowers the gravitational pull of Dark Matter and the expansion of the universe accelerates.

4.6 billion years ago, our mother star, in the Orion arm of the Milky Way galaxy, having consumed and sacrificed herself, collapsed. In the intense energy of that collapse, she was transformed into a supernova, exploding her stardust into space, and birthing all the new elements, which would take shape as Earth's body and ours.

4.5 billion years ago, that exploding stardust began to slow down, cool, and condense into a community of planets around the mother star, our Sun. Gradually, within the oceans, more complex arrangements began to take shape. These were the first simple cells, and through them, Earth awakened into life.

3.9 billion years ago, the Earth learned to take nourishment from the Sun through the process of photosynthesis. Through these simple-celled microbes, she learned to eat sunlight, to nurse from the Sun. And that dynamic laid the pattern for all future life forms, that each must receive nourishment from another, and give itself in return to become nourishment for another.

1 billion years ago, life was mysteriously drawn toward union, and the first simple-celled organisms began to reproduce sexually. Different strands of genetic memory were combined in the new offspring. This opened up infinite new possibilities. Around the same time, organisms began to feed on other organisms, and that relationship formed the basis of the community in which each would develop.

150 million years ago, the first birds took flight, and in and through them Earth broke into melody and song.

120 million years ago, the first flowering plants emerged, concentrating their life energy and memory into seed, making protein in the form of seed available for the mammals who were yet to come, and, in their flowering, bringing color and fragrance to Earth.

114 million years ago, the first placental mammals developed, warm-blooded creatures who, like the supernova, carry their unborn young within their own bodies, and who nourish them from their own substance both before and after their birth.

2.6 million years ago, the earliest hominid types evolved from the pri-

67

mate mammals in Africa. Creatures with brains and nervous systems complex enough that in and through them Earth awakened into self-conscious awareness of her existence.

70,000 years ago, our common ancestor, our great grandmother, "mitochondrial Eve" lived in Africa. There were only two thousand human beings at this time. Soon after, some of these humans began to leave Africa to populate the rest of the Earth.

Today, in this moment of grace, all humans can finally understand their common origin story, embracing and celebrating their different stories within a single Earth community in a single sacred universe. Like the Uroboros, the beginning of the Universe is like the end: each of us, right now, carries with us the memories of this story. Within us, we have the capacity to give birth to a new world.[9]

This is just an outline, a starting point, but it teaches us much. First, we begin to recognize that, through our ancestors, we are intimately connected with every one and every thing. Ancestry is not just about the past, but who we are. Our DNA is a legacy of the past, present in each of us. Learning about this basic, shared story then makes it possible to explore our more recent ancestors, which will not necessarily be shared, without the threat of its being divisive. The story of the universe is a genuine story of our connectivity and unity. We should not pretend that schools have not always tried to find such common ground. Why else to we recite the pledge of allegiance? It is certainly not a learning tool. The problem with using patriotism as a unifying concept is that it brings with it too much political baggage. Native Americans and African Americans are often uncomfortable with the patriotic narrative because it ignores their narratives. The universe story allows for each individual narrative to be honored while retaining a far more authentic sense of commonality, a common story that is no less a story than any other—that is, it is a particular version of events,

---

[9] This text was adapted from the work of Larry Edwards

not the only version—but one that derives its truth not from political or racial myths, but from our bodies and our relationship to the Earth.

Moreover, because it is based on nature, not politics, it is far more easily woven into every subject. I am not proposing a way to teach science, but a way to structure a complete curriculum. Because the way we structure a curriculum, although we are seldom aware of it, upholds a particular worldview. The worldview conveyed through the curricula of a modern school, no matter how progressive, is one of fragmentation. Each subject is disconnected from the others. The mind is disconnected from the body. Art is marginalized. A curriculum conveys meaning not merely through facts. I would not propose many new facts to be introduced to our schools. In fact, we probably have too much information. The importance in a curriculum is in how it organizes information. The story of the universe would be a narrative that would allow us to organize information fluidly, interconnectedly, organically.

HANDPRINTS ON THE WOMB

The story of the universe is not about a world that was created from the outside and that cannot be changed from within. This is the story of a universe that has changed throughout its history, and the universe itself has participated in the change. While this does not mean that we live in the mechanical, atheistic world of some modern thinkers, it does mean that we participate in the change that happens. While we cannot control our future, it is also not dictated to us. What lesson does this convey to our youth?

If we return to the human story, the reader will recall that the first humans had the courage to walk out onto the African plains. They evolved as they did because their survival depended on their spirit of exploration, their inventiveness, their intelligence, and their capacity for cooperation. They developed the ability to use symbolic language and to make meaning through symbols. Some of the earliest examples we know about are the Paleolithic cave paintings. I was lucky enough to view the paintings at Altamira, in northern Spain, during the mid-nineties. Many of the images represent the predator-prey relationship. These early people seemed to grasp intuitively that we are not in competition with nature, but that we evolve together. Had our predators not been so formidable or our prey not been so elusive, we would not have evolved the above capacities to such a degree. We owe our very existence to nature.

The other predominant image in the cave paintings is much simpler, but perhaps even more profound—the handprint. Inside the cave, these people imagined they were inside the womb and made an image that reminded them of the baby's handprints they had seen on the mother's belly. They understood, in their wisdom, that we are like the baby in the womb, pressing out at the edge of our world, exploring it, testing it. This is an important part of who we are as human beings. Not as disembodied minds, but as a part of a natural process that connects us to the living world. So, as the narrative of the universe story connects us to nature, it connects us to our role as creators, as world-builders, as mythmakers. Again, the role of nature and of creativity cannot be separated.

AN EXAMPLE FROM OUR WORK

The highlight of a recent nature retreat in Michigan was surely a midnight walk I took with a group of girls. About ten minutes from the cabin was a small lake. While many of the girls were terrified at the sheer darkness of the woods at night—this group was from Chicago—they came alive when we reached the dock. "It is so beautiful!" several of them exclaimed. I have been moved to tears by the sight of the nighttime sky, so this was something particularly gratifying to me. They were enthralled and inspired, listening intently as I explained that the light from the stars they saw had left many years ago. I am certain that they will remember it better than had they been taught it from a textbook.

It is impossible to exaggerate the importance of such an experience. This moment is the key moment in one's education. It is the moment when we are alive, when we realize that we live in a beautiful, awesome, enchanted world. We realize that, beyond what anyone else can try to force us to do, we are inspired to learn. The nature retreat is essential for students in an urban or suburban environment. We use it both as a way to begin the process and build group cohesion, and, along with the presentation of their final projects, a context for their rites of passage. We have introduced students to edible and poisonous plants and taught them how to build a fire. Invariably, we are amazed at how interested they are. In some ways, these are the easiest lessons to get ↳ ↄe students to buy into.

To summarize, the role of nature in Wisdom Education is something we should not even have to think about. But unfortunately, we must. For nature is perhaps more marginalized from school curricula than any other element of Wisdom Education. The ultimate aim should be to create an atmosphere in which children do not think about nature because it has become their basic context.

Even in science classes, our children rarely get their hands dirty, rarely get out of "the box" to truly explore their world. If the conveyance of information were the purpose of education, this would not matter. But education—Wisdom Education—is about shaping consciousness and about how we relate to and act in our world. To remove, at least partially, the barriers between the human world and the natural world, is to begin the process of shifting this relationship.

And why should we want to shift it? We should want to shift this damaged relationship because our survival as a species depends on it, for starters. The absence of nature in modern education is directly related to the ecological crisis. The modern project has been many different things, but perhaps foremost it has been a movement to forget our ecological identity. The psychological reasons for this are understandable. The wild is scary and dangerous. Our ancestors can be forgiven for believing their purpose was to tame it. But now that we have largely—by appearances—tamed nature, it is unforgiveable that we continue to pave it. Even more unforgiveable is that we continue to pave and to repress the nature in our selves. The need to bring nature into the learning process is not only practical. After all, our survival as a species is not guaranteed either way, even if it is more likely if we remember that we are a part of the Earth. The certainty is that if we can help the youth to reconnect to nature, we can promise them richer, more meaningful lives, and that they will grow up to be better educated human beings.

6 THE INTELLECT

O n the face of it, this would appear to be the least controversial chapter of this book. Who would doubt that a
major focus of education is intellectual? Indeed, Western
academia has focused on the intellect to the exclusion of all other
epistemologies. It is well worth noting here that I am advocating
neither intellectualism nor anti-intellectualism. Intellectualism is
an approach to the world that devalues epistemologies other than
the rational. From its Cartesian foundations, it holds an abstract,
disembodied approach to learning. It is an excellent way to accu-
mulate knowledge, but not so good at transforming that knowledge
into wisdom. Largely in response to the rampant intellectualism
of the modern world, an equally disturbing anti-intellectual trend
has developed in the United States. The feeling among many who
are understandably alienated from modern intellectualism is that
any form of modern learning is to be rejected. While academia becomes increasingly intellectual, churches, and frequently, the public discourse, grow increasingly anti-intellectual.

Wisdom Education advocates no such dichotomy. Instead, we
should seek to find the authentic intellect, one that recognizes how
the mind works, its relationship to the body, the psyche, and its
environment.

73

THE AUTHENTIC INTELLECT

During the Enlightenment, Western thinkers began to develop a bias for abstraction. While it is easy to criticize abstraction—and I will—let us first consider its benefits. The capacity to de-contextualize, to consider information from a theoretically "objective" perspective, has enabled us to acquire a previously unimaginable amount of information. This largely has to do with the scientific method. There are many benefits to having more information. In fact, the capacity for objectivity also can help us see alternative viewpoints. It was through this movement that democracy and the rights of the individual became widespread in the West. In short, it has expanded our world at a rapidly accelerating pace.

The problem, however, is that we have lost the capacity to see our *selves*. We have deluded ourselves into thinking that we could somehow be completely objective. This delusion has a dangerous shadow; for it has separated the human intellect from the processes of nature, eliminated the significance of the mythic in our discourse, and promoted the acquisition of fragmented knowledge without reference to the whole.

Abstraction largely comes from the notion of pure "Reason." This Enlightenment concept holds that there is a way of seeing the world without reference to one's own story, perspective, culture, or psyche. Pure Reason has nothing to do with the body or nature, but is something like a deity. Think of Aristotle's "thought thinking itself." I am not entirely critical of the concept. I write books, after all, in which I advocate ideas that I believe to be better than the ideas of certain others. There can be a fairly objective way to address these problems and that we can reach an opinion about who is right and who is wrong. To some extent, to live one's life we must make such discernments, while recognizing that we do not disagree because they are evil or stupid, but because we see these problems from different viewpoints. This is not an argument for absolute ethical relativism. But the notion that Reason is something readily attained is a dangerous idea. The European thinkers who came up with it deluded themselves into thinking that Reason was theirs alone, that they could then go about lecturing others on the way the world really is.

The truth is that the authentic intellect is not about attaining some absolute, disembodied Reason, but about cultivating one's mind to negotiate a complex matrix of (1) a brain that has evolved through natural processes (the body); (2) a mind that has been shaped by one's culture (the context); and (3) a mind that has been shaped by and shapes the interior life of the individual (the psyche). Through this matrix, the mind indeed plays the role of seeking out rational, reasonable responses to life's difficult questions. But it must do so with an acute self-awareness that remembers the complexity of this process.

The fact that the brain has evolved through natural processes speaks to our embeddedness in nature detailed in chapter 5. It is disorienting, even threatening, to most of us in the West, raised as we are on the Cartesian mind-body dualism, to think of not only our bodies but also our very thoughts to be a part of nature. But, at least in part, they are. And our study of the brain, as discussed in chapter 3, tells us that the brain has evolved to understand the world through story, through a narrative that puts information in context, not through isolated facts.

This reveals to us that we are always shaped by culture. We can, and should, try to overcome this to some extent. Radical education demands this, particularly in a culture as destructive as ours. But we never entirely overcome culture. The belief that we have overcome culture only obscures its influence, suppresses it into the shadows. It is what has led many to push back against the perceived arrogance of the elite, retreating into anti-intellectual fundamentalism.

Finally, we must know our selves just as we know facts. Each of us not only comes from a natural perspective and a cultural perspective, but from an individual and psychological perspective. That the psyche affects our ideas is hardly a radical idea. But instead of running away from this or trying to avoid the encroachment of emotion into the intellect, each of us must try to integrate our psyche into the intellect in a healthy way.

YOUNG PHILOSOPHERS

What then is the basic intellectual enterprise of Wisdom Education? To answer the question, we must remember not to slip into the utilitarianism that dominates Modern education. I have heard many well-meaning educators suggest that to teach nuanced philosophical ideas to the marginalized classes is a waste of time. These kinds of kids, the thinking goes, need to be taught practical things that will help them get jobs. Aside from the subtle racism and classism that unintentionally enters into the conversation here, there is a practical problem with the argument: no child, anywhere, at any school I know of, is learning anything in grade school, middle school, or high school that will get him a job. Few are even learning anything in college that will get them jobs. So why are we so obsessed with the future jobs of our children? Ought we not be teaching them how to think, exposing them to a broader world so they will have the capacity to know what job they might want to do and to succeed at it? What educators and, probably more to the point, politicians seem to forget when they conflate education and job-training is that being prepared for a particular job does not mean the job will exist. Factories do not close because schools have not prepared their students to work in them; they close because industries change or jobs are outsourced. Even teachers cannot find jobs teaching when the economic conditions—or decisions to spend money on the military instead of our children—lead to cuts in education budgets. The point is not that an education should not enable one to find a job. Of course it should. But whatever kind of work one does, whether one is a street sweeper or an attorney, we have failed if we cannot raise a person to think deeply about life's difficult questions.

The work of Italian Marxist philosopher Antonio Gramsci is informative here.[1] For Gramsci, schools in a true democracy should produce an "organic intellectualism" in which each individual is a

---

[1] Antonio Gramsci, *Selections from Prison Notebooks* (London: New Left Books, 1971)

philosopher, capable of critiquing and holding accountable those in government. In fact, most educational systems serve to separate a few intellectual elite from the masses who are supposed to be trained with skills to perform menial tasks. Applying the Gramscian standard to American schools reveals that we have come far short. Our intellectual elite remain detached from the lives of the masses, from nature, from their bodies, and therefore remain profoundly limited intellectually; and the masses, educated for "practical skills," are not given the skills to rule our rulers. Recall the lack of critical analysis in the lead-up to the Iraq War or the anti-intellectualism of such mass movements as the Tea Party.

This is not an argument against the practical. True philosophy integrates the intellectual and the hands-on. And this is exactly what I propose we do with our children. In the process, I believe we will do a much better job of encouraging and helping them find *meaningful* work.

Being a philosopher is not about knowing a bunch of facts, but about entering into a meaningful dialogue with our world. Knowing information is important—we cannot think critically without information—but it is only a beginning. The key is the dialogical approach. This is really something quite simple. Theodore Roszak explains, "Too much apparatus, like too much bureaucracy, only inhibits the natural flow of [the educational process]. Free human dialogue, wandering wherever the agility of the mind allows, lies at the heart of education."[2] We learn by framing arguments and listening authentically to the perspectives of others. Out of these discussions, we learn how we really feel about the world and our place in it.

Moreover, the philosopher is able to navigate the paradox. Perhaps no other type of thinking—except perhaps the emotional—has been banished from the modern classroom. The paradoxical nature of existence requires not only intelligence but also courage, for it is much easier to simply pick a side in an argument. Funda-

---

[2] Theodore Roszak, *The Cult of Information: The Folklore of Computers and the True Art of Thinking* (New York: Pantheon) 62-63.

mentalists—of religion or secularism—despise the paradox. But, as Postman puts it, "profound but contradictory ideas may exist side by side, if they are constructed from different materials and have different purposes. Each tells us something about where we stand in the universe, and it is foolish to insist that they must despise each other."[3] The most obvious example would be the debate between religion and science, dominated by fundamentalists on both sides. Our children are not taught to see the value in oppositional viewpoints, but like the cable news pundits, to pick a side and to argue without listening.

It has been my experience—having had these types of conversations with many groups of young people from various backgrounds—that the youth are yearning for this type of nuanced dialogue. They want to ask the big questions, but spend most of their time learning "useful"—to them, boring—skills. This is particularly true with marginalized groups. Because they are often behind in school, they are forced to do work that, while perhaps at their *academic* level, is far below their *intellectual* level.

In addition to the more abstract questions about what it means to be a human being and what gives our lives meaning, the philosopher must also approach questions of a more practical nature. Wisdom Education students are encouraged to explore issues going on in the world, issues in their community, and how they are interconnected. This helps the student to develop an expanded sense of community and an expanded sense of self. On a local level, because Wisdom Education emphasizes *doing*, students are then guided through a process of working to find practical solutions for problems in the community.

PEDAGOGY OF THE OPPRESSED

When I was working as an adult literacy teacher in Zimbabwe, the work of Paulo Freire had a tremendous impact on me, as it has for many who have worked with marginalized groups. *Pedagogy of the*

---

[3] Postman, p.107

Oppressed[4] is such an important work that it deserves far more than this section, but I will at least give an overview of what I feel are its key points as it pertains to this book.

The central idea of *Pedagogy of the Oppressed* is this: To truly teach the oppressed, one must not only convey information and skills; the dichotomy of teacher and student must be eliminated altogether because it only reinforces the barriers that oppress. According to Dewey, authentic education always involves a breaking down of the barriers, or even reversal of the roles, of teacher and student: "The teacher is a learner, and the learner is, without knowing it, a teacher." Freire uses the "banking" metaphor to describe modern education: "Education becomes an act of depositing, in which the students are the depositories and the teacher is the depositor. Instead of communicating, the teacher issues communiqués and makes deposits and the students patiently receive, memorize, and repeat."[5] The antithesis of this is "problem-posing" education, in which people begin to challenge their place in the world and how it came to be, seeing the world as dynamic rather than static.

For Freire, this can only done through "*conscientizacao*," the critical consciousness that allows the individual to recognize the injustices of society and believe that she can play an active role in overcoming them.[6] *Conscientizacao* is threatening not only to the oppressor, but also to the oppressed; for, according to Freire, many oppressed people have become afraid of the freedom it promises. It requires one to transform one's self-perception from that of an object—one who is only acted upon—to that of a subject, one who knows and acts. In our subjectivity, we believe we have something to say about the world and can change it.[7]

Freire wrote about the very kind of program in which I worked in Zimbabwe—adult literacy—and it is perhaps more straightforward to suggest that we encounter another adult on equal terms.

---

[4] Paulo Freire, *Pedagogy of the Oppressed* (New York, Penguin, 1993)

[5] Ibid., p.72

[6] Ibid., p. 17

[7] Ibid., p.18.

But what about children? How can we convey to our youth, particularly the marginalized, that we respect them while recognizing the need to instill in them a respect for their elders? This requires a delicate balance that can only be developed in the relationships between student and teacher.

One way is to provide an appropriate time for students to find mistakes with the teacher, with a book, or with something they have seen in the world. The student must, however, be encouraged not only to complain, but also to state her case in a way that shows real reflection.

For critical consciousness to truly occur on a profound level—as opposed to mere critical thinking—the student and teacher must enter into an exploration of the narratives that define them and give them their place in the world. Each of us—teachers included—must ask ourselves, "What are the stories that tell us who we are?" "Who is telling my story, and why?" A student of mine who is a high school dropout, for example, put together a list of reasons, assumptions, or stories about him that are commonly held in our society. We found that many were false, and all were incomplete or exaggerated. The challenge of the student, then, is to create a counter-narrative, a new story that places him in the world on his own terms. If we do not tell our own story, someone else will.

For Freire, as for the programs I have run, a key component in teaching the oppressed is to allow them to create a narrative about their world and their experiences in it. This is one of the key roles of creative expression in the educational process. It can be a healing experience for the individual, the community, and a people. Creativity can plan a crucial role here because it can allow for students who have not yet developed the verbal or academic skills to express themselves through other media, particularly visual media, on which Freire placed special emphasis. Many of the myths we teach our children—particularly today with the predominance of television—are conveyed visually. Given the opportunity to create an image that defines themselves or their community, the youth can subvert the images to which they have been exposed through the mass media. But to do this requires not only delicate brush of the painter, but also the sharp sword of the intellect.

THE SWORD OF WISDOM

The authentic intellect is the sword of wisdom. While I have described in detail how Wisdom Education requires more than mere intellectualism and facts, it does not mean that we should be anti-intellectual. Far too often, I have observed those who wish to critique Modernity, the West, or the intellectual elite reduce themselves to anti-intellectualism that rejects critical thinking and even makes up facts. While I am well aware of the complexities of various epistemological approaches and the danger of thinking in terms of a dualism of "the way things really are" as opposed to everyone else's ignorance, we must provide our youth with an epistemological approach that is more rigorous, not less, than in modern education. That is to say that, while modern education provides our young people with many facts, it does not provide them with the intellectual tools to discern which facts are valuable and which facts we should accept. Our students are neither trained nor encouraged to challenge the ideas that are put before them.

An obvious place to start is a rigorous media awareness curriculum. More than ever, our youth grow up in an environment saturated with media. According to Neil Postman, the average child will see 500,000 television commercials, "which means that the television commercial is the most substantial source of values to which the young are exposed."[8] And the degree to which this saturation is occurring is increasing at a rapidly accelerating pace. I am still in my thirties—my own childhood was not that long ago—but I am regularly amazed at the possibilities for a child to be exposed to media. Parents are simply unequipped to cope with it. Like me, they do not recall having their time spent in front of a screen being monitored aggressively. This is because the options were few: four or five television channels, with only a few hours of programming

---

[8] Postman, p.33

a week that would interest a child at all. Parents must deal with video games, round-the-clock children's programming, and the internet, to name the most prevalent mass media lures. Consequently, as most parents—like their parents before them—have let children watch as much television and spend as much time on the internet (even to the point of carrying the internet around with them in the form of a smart phone) as they want, while limiting their free- and outside-time, our children are constantly plugged in.

The developmental and cognitive problems associated with this phenomenon are the greatest danger to our children. These cannot be dealt with intellectually. No media awareness campaign can recover our children's emotional well-being or our society's connection to nature. But we can—we must—at least help our children think critically about the images they are given. As I have stated before, the television is now the fire around which we sit, where we hear the stories that give us our values. Children do not question these stories because they are so immersed in them, just as children in times past would never have questioned the town preacher.

To question the mass media not only helps us deal with those images. It also gives our children the intellectual tools to create their own images. If we take seriously the role of our youth in creating values through their creativity, we must require that they do more than simply "stay off the streets" while they are producing their art. We want their art to be transformative—both for themselves and for their world. This requires the sword of intellect—to look at the stories and images they have been given and to look at their own work deeply and critically.

Because of our values and the core metaphors that inform them, we think of the intellect in a profoundly limited way. Most of us think of the world in terms of smart and dumb people, just as there are those who are creative and those who are not creative. The I.Q. test, for example, is accepted as an objective, undeniable definition of one's intelligence. This is rooted in the emergence of the Enlightenment worldview that led us to think of learning as the acquisition of quantifiable and measurable facts. Genius, originally one's particular gifts,[9] came to mean only one particular form of intellect. The notion of testing and quantifying this capacity came about with the industrial revolution and the beginnings of modern psychology. Industrialism intensified the mechanistic metaphor that held that the human body, like the natural world, was a machine that could be understood and tested. Science, in its objectivism and penchant for the quantifiable, was unlocking t! ᴧ ɪnysteries of nature; with Freud, psychology began to understand the mind through the scientific lens. There were only two forms of intelligence that mattered: the ability to memorize facts and the capacity for deductive reasoning.

On a typical test, including an IQ test, there is no opportunity for the child to provide a narrative, to explain the reasons for an answer. At times, a wrong answer could reveal a more profound intelligence than a correct one. But we are so concerned with the reductive, Modern notion of "scientific" truth that we have ignored the deeper truths—the wisdom—that a narrative can reveal. This unwillingness to hear the narrative of the child is connected to our "zero-tolerance" disciplinary codes, our punitive school cultures that blame those who suffer from our failed system.

The notion of "multiple intelligences"[10] posits that there are many ways we can be intelligent, that, in fact, the intellect is more about discovering our particular gifts than it is about conforming to a prescribed test or set of standards With all the talk about "standards" in education, no one ever seems to question what those standards are. This is because we assume that we all know what intelligence is—but the intellect is actually impossible to quantify. The authentic intellect integrates emotion, creativity, logic, and more.

---

[9] Originally meaning "deity of generation or birth"—i.e. something we all possess—it came to mean a "person of outstanding intellectual ability" during the Enlightenment. John Ato, *Dictionary of Word Origins* (New York: Arcade, 1990) p. 252.

[10] Howard Gardner, *Multiple Intelligences: New Horizons in Theory and Practice* (New York: Basic Books, 1993)

The task, therefore, of the educator, is to *educe*—to draw out a wisdom that is already present in each of us, a wisdom that is at once unique and universal. This is the original meaning of education.

In Wisdom Education, there remains a special role for the intellectual capacity for rational discourse. We need to be able to think critically and abstractly, as long as we can remember that this is not all there is to the intellect. Reason cannot be all there is to the intellect, because reason does not exist on its own. The mind exists in concert with body and soul.

But even this nuanced and complex view of the intellect does not necessarily lead to wisdom. Wisdom arises in the cultural ecosystem that allows one's mind to bring forth ideas, emotional responses, and dialogues that are meaningful. The intellect's role, in part, is to assess value. But value—and wisdom—comes forth in community, in collaboration, and in the application of an idea.

7

THE BODY

The Western world has a strange relationship with the human body. On the one hand, we seem obsessed with it. Advertisements constantly tell our youth how inadequate their bodies are; sexuality is self-righteously critiqued and shamelessly sold. On the other hand, we have banished the body from realms of human experience other than the commercial, including education. Perhaps this is because the commercialization of the body is so important in our consumerist culture. Nonetheless, a comprehensive wisdom must integrate the body into the educational process just as it incorporates nature; for to understand ourselves and our place in the world requires that we educate the whole person, including the body.

Just as we have increasingly kept our children inside, away from nature, we have also reduced their physical activity. As pressure has mounted to increase the test scores in basic skills, school children spend less and less time at physical education and recess. While what goes on in most gym classes is not exactly what I am talking about in terms of integrating the body into the learning process, it is still a shame that young people have less physical activity. Obesity rates have skyrocketed owing as much to this lack of exercise as to poor diets. And, ironically, evidence suggests that physical activity actually improves academic outcomes.

But more than for any of these reasons, we should integrate the body into the educational process because our bodies are part of who we are and how we experience the world. While it has become a truism to suggest that we are "not our bodies," the truth is more nuanced. To understand it, it is worth exploring the roots of the radical separation of mind and body in Western culture.

THE RADICAL SEPARATION

The radical separation of mind and body has its roots in some of the seminal thinkers and concepts in Western culture. As with many core ideas in Western philosophy, we can begin with Plato, who was among the earliest to articulate—whether it was originally his idea is another matter—the idea of a soul that is distinct from the body. In the *Phaedo*, he suggests that the soul (Gr. *psyche*) is immortal—and therefore "real"—whereas the body, because it is temporal, is not real.

This concept became influential in the development of Christian theology. Augustine of Hippo, the most prominent early Christian theologian, was deeply influenced by Plato and, while he eventually rejected the Manichaean teaching that held that the natural world is corrupt, Platonic and Manichaean dualism remained embedded in his thought.

In spite of the continued presence of a certain Augustinian line of thinking in Christian theology that rejects the body, it was not until the secular philosophical movement known as the Enlightenment that the definitive line was drawn between body and mind (or soul). Drawing from Descartes, Modern thinkers now believed that what was most fundamental to a human being was one's thoughts. The body was considered at best separate from the true self, at worst corrupt and degraded.

It was out of this paradigm that some of the core metaphors of Modernity arose. The body, like nature, was understood to be a machine. It was not far from being considered a commodity as well.

When the modern school came about, it was all too obvious that the mind, not the body, was to be the focus. "Whenever I get the urge to exercise," said Robert Hutchins, former President of the University of Chicago, "I lie down until the feeling passes away." This attitude—that using the body was somehow *beneath* the educated person—clearly had classist implications. But they would not have been expressed in this way without already assuming that body and mind were fundamentally separate.

Recently, however, a new vision—or perhaps, a recapitulation of an old one—of the human has come forth. Medicine, psychology, and cognitive science now understand the human being as an interconnected whole. The physician realizes that healing requires dealing with the psychological as well as the physical; the emerging field of somatic psychology treats the emotions through the body. And, as described earlier, cognitive science recognizes that our thoughts are connected to the physical processes of the brain, processes that have arisen out of evolutionary, chemical, and biological processes.

All this is not to reduce one's thoughts to brain chemistry. No scientist has come anywhere close to explaining a Dostoevsky novel, a Coltrane album, or a Martin Luther King, Jr. speech in terms of chemistry. It is telling, however, that the worldview based upon fragmentation has now revealed to us a holism that, while not entirely quantifiable, can be described with a newfound precision. If even those most committed to fragmentation admit that the human is best understood holistically, how can we argue?

With this vision of the human in mind, how do we integrate the body into the learning process? It is far easier to recognize the importance of the body than to have this importance reflective in a system—the Modern school—designed to ignore it. The remainder of this chapter will be devoted to a few suggestions.

SILENCE AS TEACHER
THE CONTEMPLATIVE ELEMENT OF EDUCATION

The previous chapter was mostly about things we can talk about.

Most of us, if we are to think about how we have been educated, will likely think of the verbal—lectures, discussions, writing, taking tests, reading. There is no place for silence in modern education. Indeed, there is no place for silence in modern life. While we probably do not spend any more time than ever in direct, face-to-face conversation, the rest of our waking hours is filled with an ever-ready cell phone connection, a television that never turns off.

Silence means more than just quiet, although that would be a good start. Reading, while surely an important aspect of education, is still verbal, and therefore not true silence. Silence requires not merely the quieting of the mouth, but also of the mind.

The proliferation of distractions like television and cell phones has inhibited our ability to be present. We are always looking for the next list to make, the next video to watch, the next gossip to spread. Even on those rare moments when we are not "plugged-in," the mind continues to be distracted. We no longer feel the wind blowing through our hair, the sun warming our face. We are seldom present to our bodies. The Manichaean dualism that arose millennia ago has manifested itself in a strange paradox: in our belief that only the mind is "real" we have come to believe that false realities are realer than the trees, the sun, or our own bodies. Is not "reality TV" evidence that we have lost touch with the real?

Silence—the practice of meditation—is nothing new. It is practiced in different forms in most of the world's great cultural traditions. Its practice is a clear example of the non-duality of body and mind. For, although it is a practice of quieting the mind, it is a practice that begins and ends with the body. To meditate requires no adherence to any set of ideas. It requires us to attempt to let go of ideas. The form it takes, then, is dependent upon what we do with our bodies. Some practices require standing, others sitting. Breathing techniques differ. There is no "goal" in meditation, but it is possible to say that we have achieved some measure of "success" (I am well aware that this kind of language is highly problematic in reference to meditation) when we become aware and accepting of our bodies.

My own experience with teaching meditation to youth has been mixed. Some young people are extremely open; others are obstinately resistant. Simplicity generally works better—sitting and counting the breath has been received better than complex Qigong practices, in my experience. In some cases, the silence is threatening, even scary.

Silence is also extremely important in cultivating a connection to nature. Silent walks allow us to awaken our senses to the living world of which we are a part.

Many meditative experiences are active. In Matthew Fox's graduate school program, "Art-as-meditation" was a regular part of every class. When we are creative, particularly when we are making something with our hands, we enter into a meditative state as we are fully focused on the subject of our creativity. And, as the poet and potter M.C. Richards points out, art is *bodily*. We are making something with our hands, not just thinking and talking. For Richards, the focus of the potter on her wheel is similar to the Buddhist focus on the breath in meditation.[1]

Silence is only one step in reintegrating the body into education. Young people need to move just as they need silence. In some cases, students will be more open to silence and meditation if it is part of a more active practice. And just as with meditation, there is no need to come up with something completely new. The ancient practice of martial arts can provide an activity that allows students to get exercise as well as find some measure of silence.

MARTIAL ARTS

As with meditative and contemplative practice, a rich tapestry of cultural traditions is available in the practice and study of martial arts. To learn a martial art is not merely to learn to fight, but also to immerse oneself in a tradition, a lineage. It can open children up to the diversity of various cultures or further root them in their own heritage.

---

[1] M.C. Richards, *Centering in Poetry and Pottery* (Wesleyan University Press, 1989)

Any physical activity can promote health and fitness. Having been an athlete as a child and throughout high school and college, I have drawn great satisfaction from various sports. In fact, I love sports and will continue to watch them and play them throughout my life. So I am not opposed to sports. However, my encounter with the Taoist-based martial art of Bagua as described in chapter 1 has led me to the conviction that martial arts is actually a better teaching tool than any sport.

The most obvious reason to learn martial arts is self-defense. There are practical reasons why one might want to be able to defend oneself or one's family against an attack. Unfortunately, ours is a violent world. To be a young, black man, or homosexual, or a woman, makes one a target. While martial arts do not guarantee immunity from violence—I have not yet heard of a technique to stop a bullet—it can help someone avoid serious harm. I have seen young people gain tremendous confidence from knowing they have a little bit of skill in defending themselves. Confidence and empowerment are crucial skills in teaching the marginalized, for they have often been made to feel powerless.

Admittedly, becoming a better fighter is not the best path to non-violence. Many will object that teaching martial arts only encourages violence. This, however, would be to ignore the majority of martial arts teaching—of which fighting is only a part.

A key aspect to martial arts is discipline. While other sports can involve discipline, it is not inherent to sports. For example, when I played basketball, I never learned the art of discipline. That is, while some discipline is obviously required to learn any skill, living a disciplined life was optional. Some coaches may encourage it; others may not. More often than not, "discipline" involves a lot of yelling and punishment, but not much instilling of a truly disciplined life. In martial arts, one learns to deal not only with external adversaries, but also with the internal challenges that arise in the process of learning something new. In this way, martial artists can teach us not only the specific skills of the art, but also the way to live a disciplined life that allows us to learn more of everything.

For example, one simple but important discipline one learns in martial arts is the ability to remain calm in stressful or chaotic situations. Regardless of one's technique or skills, remaining calm can be the key to emerging from a physical conflict without injury. But this discipline can be carried over to other aspects of one's life. So often, capable students harm their own ability to succeed in school by frequently losing their temper. Recent research has shown that students who do poorly on tests are often hindered by society's beliefs about them. Meditation has shown to mitigate this effect.[2]

Every practice or combat technique learned in martial arts has a peaceful corollary. The circular movements of Bagua can teach the student how to deal with problems in a less confrontational way; the reversal of movement teaches us the paradoxical nature of our world.

Along with discipline, there is also an ethics of authentic martial arts practice that discourages needless violence. The martial artist does not have to call on an external ethical system to determine right and wrong, because part of the skill of the martial artist is the avoidance of conflict. Just as we avoid an opponent's kick, we avoid the violent confrontation altogether. At the same time, we learn the courage to defend against injustice or bullying. No sport has such an ethical component. The recent controversy of steroids in baseball demonstrates this perfectly. I am making no judgment on those who took steroids. In fact, I believe it would be inappropriate to do so. For there was never any ethic in baseball, or any sport, that required anything but a win-at-all-costs mentality.

It has also been my experience that martial arts can be a key to getting the youth to meditate. Sitting meditation is often—not always—hard to sell. Young people often need to move and they

---

[2] Recent studies have shown that perceptions of one's ethnic group can have an effect on test scores, regardless of one's ability or even the degree to which one believes in those perceptions. Meditation has been proven to mitigate these effects. See Sian Beilock, *Choke: What the Secrets of the Brain Reveal about Getting it Right When you Have To* (New York: Simon & Schuster, 2010)

often want to see a purpose behind what they are doing. They can more easily grasp why one would learn martial arts and its practical application than meditation. And meditation is, of course, a key part of any authentic martial arts practice.

Through all these practices, particularly the meditation, martial arts can instill in the student a deeper awareness. Becoming aware of one's surroundings, one's body, and one's connection to others allows a shift in consciousness and attitude that is fundamental to radical education. This speaks to the importance of the body: truly radical education requires an awareness that shifts consciousness, an awareness that can be cultivated with embodied practices like martial arts. The modern student, more than any student in the history of school, has difficulty with focus and concentration due to distractions such as television.

While I am not a martial arts teacher, I do have enough skill and the blessing of my own teacher to convey some of it to my students. As my teacher used to say, "I don't want you to become great martial artists; I want you to become great teachers." What he meant was that the most important thing was to learn a practice and share that practice with others, not how many people one can beat up.

UNPLUGGING THE FALSE UMBILICAL CORD

Go somewhere young people hang out. You will notice something very strange. They will all have wires hanging from their ears and be staring at a screen, "texting" furiously. There will be little eye contact and even less conversation. No one touches one another. I cannot prove it, but I suspect that when those whom they are texting are actually present, they will not talk much to them either.

Technology is not necessarily good or bad, but it is always powerful. It can turn our world upside down. The youth's addiction to such useless technology is not their fault: in indulging them, in buying them all this useless junk, we have truly failed them. Could there be a more obvious—or sad—testament to the rejection of the body than children who send thousands of text messages a day but have no conversations? Our youth play more video games than sports. They believe a Facebook page to be a more real representation of their identity than their own bodies. Two of my students once got into a fight over something written on a Facebook page. The attachment to such addictive technologies can be dealt with only by disciplined adults. The youth will scream and shout when you deny them a new phone or video game or force them to turn off the television—indeed they will act as though you are severing an umbilical cord, their attachment to "reality," the only world they know—but we must. For when we do cut it, it at least opens up the possibility of awakening the senses, of returning to our bodies. Part of the problem here is that, for parents, the umbilical cord metaphor is even deeper. They believe that they are more "connected" to their children, and that their children are safer, through this technology. The problem is that it is such a superficial connection. And the safety they seek is, first of all, false, and secondly, seeks to overcome a "danger" based largely on paranoia.

While parents are the most important actors in this problem, teachers also play an important role. Most do not allow cell phone or such devices in their classrooms and understand how distracting they are. Teachers are less aware, however, of the difficulties with incorporating technologies into the classroom. As I have said before, I am not against using technology altogether. We must remember, however, that the body is a part of the learning process. If a technology can be used without compromising the role of the body, it should be used. Too often, however, technologies are employed for a short-term benefit that ultimately leads to more disembodied and disconnected sensibility in the students.

HEALTHY BODIES, HEALTHY PLANET

A healthy student will be happier and more ready to learn than one who is obese or sick. This involves not only physical activity, but also diet and environmental factors. Students who eat fast food will remain unhealthy and unfocused, regardless of how much exercise they get. Students living in polluted areas will have such ailments as asthma at a greater rate. Health, and the body, does not end at the skin. A deeper awareness of the body can and should lead to deeper connection to nature and our ecosystem. The body is a part of nature.

An ecological sensibility is deeply connected to our attitudes toward the body. The narrative of the Universe story teaches us that the body arises from the elements of the Earth and from the web of relationships of the ecosystem. In order to move beyond the modern industrial worldview, an Earth wisdom must be brought forth that reflects this truth.

I should also make clear that I am not advocating, nor have I ever taught, a martial arts class, or a meditation class. I am proposing that such practices become a part of a holistic learning experience. Any class can begin with meditation. Meditation can calm the class and help students process what they have learned; using the body can keep students from being bored and distracted.

In general, every class I teach involves some sort of meditation and some physical activity. Instead of sending students to computers or watching videos, why not send them outside? Wisdom Education is not about adding new subjects, but about eradicating subjects and integrating the essential elements of our humanity into the educational process. In every educational endeavor there is a role for the body. Indeed, there is nothing we can learn without the body.

The body largely plays a role in the modern school of something that hinders learning. In part, this has to do many of the misconceptions of the Modern worldview, *i.e.* that learning is about the disembodied mind alone. In a very real way, however, the body can inhibit learning. When our youth are in poor health and cannot concentrate due to their diets and lack of exercise, it can be difficult for them to focus. Moreover, our alienation from the natural world leaves many distracted and unaware. But there is a way that the body can be a benefit to the educational process. When we recognize the whole person, the body plays an important and integral role. In addition to body and mind, this also must involve the soul.

8 THE SOUL

As with the subject of values, many will object to this chapter on the grounds that soul should be something discussed in church, or at home, but not at school. This chapter is not about any religious dogma, however. Rather, it is a recognition that human experience cannot be reduced to the body and the mind. Emotions are as important as ideas; education is as much about creating a happy child as a healthy and intelligent one. Indeed, mental, physical, and emotional health are part of the whole person, who should be the subject of education.

"Soul" is a word that escapes facile definitions. At times, we use it to refer to emotional and spiritual depth, to a way of being in the world that cannot be reduced to the intellectual. In Western religion, the soul refers to the non-physical element that makes up the individual. The original, Greek word for soul was "*psyche*," from which we get the field of psychology.[1]

The concept of maladjustment among our youth in the title of this book speaks to the social and psychological problems that af-

---

[1] For more on the soul, see my book *Cosmosophia: Cosmology, Mysticism, and the Birth of a New Myth* (Hiraeth Press, 2011)

flict our youth. There is evidence that mental illness is increasing in our society.[2] Our children are increasingly depressed. The answer, primarily, has been an increased focused on the mental and emotional problems of the depressed individual. Psychotherapy and, disturbingly, drugs have ever been more commonly applied to our children. As usual, however, we seem to have missed the broader context for our malaise. Modernity has left us without a myth or the rites of passage that bind us to one another and fits us into the world. We are increasingly lost and alienated; our youth increasingly turn to drugs (which is no surprise considering we prescribe them so readily), technology, and consumerism to find an ever-elusive meaning in their lives. The problem, as Dr. King teaches us, is not that we need to focus on the individual child's failure to conform to a society that gives her no meaning; we must create a society that provides a context for a child to live a meaningful life.

That there is a therapeutic component to learning should surprise no one who has worked with children, or any age group, actually. We bring our emotional state and our experiences to the process. And if we are experiencing extreme trauma, we will have trouble learning. The soul should be addressed because we must deal with our emotions as part of the learning process.

But I would like to avoid reducing the soul to modern psychology. While therapy can be an important part of helping one through the healing and self-awareness that is a part of Wisdom Education, there is a greater role for the soul. The soul speaks to a way of being in the world that requires depth and asking questions of one's self. The soul is one's individual interiority, so it requires one to ask of one's self, "who am I?" This is a question that must be asked and answered in several ways: consulting with elders; studying ancestral traditions; learning what the great spiritual traditions have said; therapeutic work and reflection; and engaging in authentic rites of passage. In each case, the basic questions posed intellectually in chapter 6 must be addressed spiritually in order to not only

---

[2] See Ken Robinson, *Out of our Minds*

think differently about the world, but also to actually transform one's self and one's world together.

WHO AM I?

In some ways, this is the central question of Wisdom Education. One could argue that it is the central question of our lives as human beings. For all the time we spend worried about finances and careers, about what to buy and what to wear, our ultimate happiness lies in having a sense of who we are—that is, finding purpose and meaning and a sense of our place in the world.

The problems of Modernity are mirrored in Modern education. We cannot blame educators for reflecting, to some degree, their society. Foremost among these problems is the loss of a sense of identity that binds us to one another and to our world. In letting go of the restrictions of traditional society that "kept us in our place," we have also lost a sense of belonging. I am not arguing for a return to a more restrictive, traditional culture—this is what the fundamentalist argues—but to remember that making our lives meaningful is important work.

In exalting the individual, modern industrial society gives us remarkable individual freedoms. The problem is that we are so individualistic, at times, that we forget that we owe our existence to a web of relationships. The point is not to eradicate the individual, as some fundamentalists, New Age cults, and totalitarian regimes advocate, but to situate the individual in a meaningful story. These groups fixate on texts; I am emphasizing *con*text.

I want all of my students to find some measure of personal success. I want them to find financial stability and the prestige that comes from a good job and degrees. But this cannot be the basis for an educational system, for these achievements are competitive. They reflect a society with winners and losers. The "Race to the Top"[3] cannot be anything but a reflection of this ethic. In all the

[3] This is the title of a recent U.S. Department of Education Program in which states with more innovative ways to improve outcomes (test scores) received extra money from the federal government.

talk about test scores, it is seldom mentioned that tests are graded in terms of a percentile—this means our success, as in every other realm, is based upon how we compete with each other. I have not yet heard it explained how we will have every child in America scoring in the 99th percentile. Perhaps this, as much as any test, shows how bad Americans have become at mathematics.

So what of the child who does not go to Harvard? What do we want from a person, in this culture, of whom it can be said, "He is educated"? It is my hope that the answers to this question emerge, in part, from this book as a whole. That is, a person who is educated is creative, has a relationship with nature and the body, tries to be healthy of mind and of spirit, is intellectually astute and thinks critically, and does something meaningful and useful with all these capacities. The answer cannot come from a single person or a single book. It must emerge as part of a holistic process. Many of the answers will emerge from the youth themselves.

At the core of any answer one might come up with, however, is the answer to this simple question: "*Who am I?*" It is a question I pose to my students throughout my time with them, in various ways. We watch how it evolves, as it should, as they grow and learn. It is a question that requires a relationship, first, with one's self. Students must practice silence and be comfortable enough with them selves to ask the difficult questions. But it also has to do with one's creative expression. Indeed, it is a question that can only be answered through the mythic, poetic voice. Through our art, we all define our selves. If we watch a music video today, we find what many women think of them selves, what many people of color think of them selves. These ideas come from a society that has marginalized them, has devalued them. The task of an educator then, is to find a way to identify our selves that does not rely on society's skewed ideas.

For any modern person, whether on the margins or very much in the mainstream, the tendency is to define oneself individualistically. Descartes' ideas—*cogito ergo sum* ("I think therefore I am")—form the basis for modern self-definition. This philosophy negates the body, the Earth, our cultural traditions, our communities, our ancestors, and our interpersonal relationships. Modern education has done more than simply omit the soul and the emotions: by forcing the student to abstract, to separate the interiority from the object of study—indeed, to separate the interiority from *everything*, even that which gives the individual a core identity, like a culture—education is experienced, on an emotional level, as *loneliness*. When the Nobel Prize winning physicist Steven Weinberg says, "the more the universe seems comprehensible, the more it also seems pointless," he is revealing a truth about modern epistemology more than about the nature of the cosmos.

This chapter is about how to find meaning in one's life in the context of one's relationships, not in what the philosopher Alan Watts referred to as "the skin-encapsulated ego." This requires not only feeling better about our selves—the work of psychotherapy—but also expanding our sense of self. As it turns out, the answer to the question "Who am I?" involves the whole world, past, present, and future.

THE ANCESTORS

When Matthew Fox entered the Wisdom Education Movement, he used the acronym "A.W.E.," which stood for Ancestral Wisdom Education.[4] He did so, in part, because he advocated a return, in a modern context, to the kind of education our ancestors would have had.

The ancestors also play a much deeper role in Wisdom Education. Physically, we are our ancestors. Our DNA is an embodied memory of their legacy. Our ancestors connect us to our specific cultural traditions. Young people, particularly African-Americans, can be empowered by learning about their own, rich heritage. In our efforts to create a new, American culture, we have placed far

---

[4] Matthew Fox, *The A.W.E. Project, Reinventing Education, Reinventing the Human* (Westminster John Knox Press, 2006)

too much emphasis on forgetting our past. For some, the past holds painful memories. After all, we were not all kings and queens. But to remember and come to terms with such a history can also be empowering, for it can be a way to deal with struggles and shame we may hold in this lifetime.

Moreover, the ancestors bind us to a broader world. We are connected to every other person on the planet—in a scientifically provable and embodied way—through our DNA. What are the ethical consequences of this knowledge? Our ethics has to do with how we answer the question "Who am I?" When we answer the question in terms of an isolated self, anything goes. When we answer in terms of a family that we know, we are likely to treat those with whom we feel connected—family members, countrymen, etc.—better than others. When we remember that we share an ancestry with every other person, the answer to the question is changed dramatically. We realize that our fate is inextricably connected to that of others.

But we do not merely share genes with every person on the planet; we share genes with every living being. Our attitude toward other living beings, therefore, can be transformed through this knowledge. That is to say, this knowledge can change our behavior if we transform the knowledge into wisdom. This means we must not only know the facts, but also use those facts to transform our self-definition. Knowledge of the world becomes knowledge of self; and knowledge of self becomes knowledge of the world. Put together, this is wisdom.

THE WORLD'S GREAT WISDOM TRADITIONS

Part of studying our ancestors should be learning about how they answered life's most difficult questions. What do traditional African cultures, or Hindus, or Muslims say about what it means to be human? Many will object: "Isn't this teaching religion in schools?" For some reason, many people believe that because we cannot advocate a particular religion in school—i.e., proselytize—that religion cannot be mentioned. This ridiculous assertion, stemming from a fear of offending the closed-minded, has resulted in a populace that is shockingly ignorant about religion.[5] Can anyone who has endured post-911 America not recognize this as a problem?

I am not advocating any particular religion, but I am advocating asking our children to think about some of the questions that religion—at its best—has sought to answer. Why not see what some of these traditions have said? While many of its critics have pointed out the closed-mindedness and violence associated w· h religion, this is only one side to a complex human endeavor. For all the benefits of Modernity—the freedoms, the material benefits, the knowledge—we still have some of the same basic needs that religion once provided for us. Fundamentalism, which is the form of religion most often in the news and referred to by critics of religion *writ large*, provides meaning if we abandon our critical faculties; liberal religion lacks the emotional, soulful aspect of traditional religions.

History and current events cannot be learned without understanding the basic beliefs of other cultures. Intellectually and emotionally, our youth can learn a great deal from digging deeper into those traditions. I am not talking about learning the Five Pillars or the Ten Commandments, but th fundamental assumptions and values of these great traditions. By looking at how others have answered those questions, we can begin to answer them for ourselves.

THE THERAPEUTIC ELEMENT OF EDUCATION

Education must involve healing if it is to work at all. Most educators will recognize that many of our children do poorly at school because they have been traumatized. To some extent, this brings us to an area that cannot be dealt with in the school. That is, for the most part, a school or after school program cannot make a child's home life much better. But we can integrate into the learning process a healing element, one that does not require a student to misbehave to grant the space to talk about feelings.

If a child comes to school hungry, we would not punish him for being unable to concentrate. But when a child us unable to deal

---

[5] A recent Pew Forum poll indicated that Americans know very little about religion, in spite of our religiousness. http://pewforum.org/other-beliefs-and-practices/u-s-religious-knowledge-survey.aspx

with conflict due to traumatic circumstances, he will undoubtedly be punished. This is not the fault of the teacher. Because the normal classroom has no space for the emotions, a child who cannot deal with his emotions will be removed, punished, and stigmatized. The cycle of trauma and punishment prepares this child for nothing but prison.

Part of the healing I am calling for comes in the form of the meditative practice I put forth in chapter 7. Teaching a regular practice to deal with stress, anger, depression, and other emotions should be part of any Wisdom Education program. In addition to teaching these individual practices, we have run boys and girls groups, led by trained facilitators, to provide a space for the students to talk about their feelings. Although this is less embodied and more verbal than meditation, it is similar in that there is little content introduced. It is more about how we feel than introducing new ideas. These groups, like meditation, are for all students, not just those who have been labeled in some way.

There is still room, of course, for individual therapy. The idea is not to remove such services, but to integrate a therapeutic component into the normal curriculum so that students can have help dealing with their emotions and integrate them in a balanced and healthy way into their intellectual and creative endeavors.

TOWARD AUTHENTIC RITES OF PASSAGE

In recent years, the term "Rites of Passage" has been en vogue in our schools. Instead of "graduation," some schools now have rite of passage ceremony. The ceremonies themselves have changed little—except that, unlike when I was a child and the only really big ceremony was high school graduation, there is a sort of graduation ceremony every year.

What happens in schools at the end of the year is not what I am talking about here. Such ceremonies are fine, but they do not constitute what I am calling *authentic* Rites of Passage. To understand what I mean by this term, we—and this includes our students—will have to explore our ancestral traditions.

Every traditional culture I know of had some kind of rite of passage. Rites of passage take many forms, and involve the passage from one type of being, one particular role in a community, to another. Birth, the cutting of the umbilical cord, is the prime example, and impossible to purge due to its necessity, as much as we have tried to medicalize and desacralize it. Birth is a transformation not only for the birthed, but for birther as well. We are transformed into parents in the process. The wedding, perhaps more than any other modern ceremony, remains a common rite of passage, frequently regarded as sacred. But we must remember that it remains so common largely because of the extent to which it has become a commercial industry.

The entrance into adulthood, however, once the most important rite of passage, is almost non-existent in the modern world. Even the ceremonies that do remain—like the bar mitzvah—are often more about getting gifts that becoming an adult. Formerly, these ceremonies were so significant because, in leading the child through puberty and into adulthood, they taught us how to become a full-fledged human being in a particular culture. They answered the question, "Who am I?" teaching an individual how he belonged.

In the absence of such ceremonies, many of the youth have resorted to such alternatives as gang initiations. In the absence of authentic, healthy communities, our youth find belonging in bastardized rites of passage into cults of violence and dysfunction. Much has been said about the lack of role models in some of our communities and its effect on our young men. It is certainly true that our streets are filled with boys in men's bodies. But I would argue that even when men are present they have little idea about how to facilitate a boy's entrance into manhood. Indeed, Wall Street is among the streets I refer to as filled with little boys, and surely most of *those* men had fathers around. We require not only men, but also deep and meaningful—authentic—rites of passage for our boys to become men.

There is a desire we all possess for the darkness. In Western civilization, coming from a long tradition, we have shunned the darkness, avoided it as though it were not a part of us. Darkness, in our dualistic cosmology, has come to be equated with evil. In our avoidance of the darkness, we have shunned the depth and struggle that should be a part of any authentic rite of passage. Even birth, the mother of all rites of passage, has come to be sanitized with drugs. Our youth are yearning for depth. If we do not help them journey into the darkness, where genuine creativity can begin, they will find it on their own in destructive ways.

In Wisdom Education, the rite of passage should be based partly on tradition and the essentially human pattern of the coming-of-age ritual, and partly on the specific needs and interests of the group. Traditionally, the rite of passage had to do with leaving the comfort zone of the community and maternal protection. For our students, this involves a retreat in which students have time to connect to nature and to go through a process that forces them to deal with adversity. During the retreat, students have time for silent reflection; they learn survival techniques; they endure long hikes in difficult terrain. Students learn about edible plants and prepare food. Moreover, they reflect on the entire year in girls and boys groups.

The specifics of the rite of passage ceremony can be determined by the group. Sometimes, this has to do with its own cultural traditions. There are, however, several components that are held in common with almost all authentic rites of passage.

The first component is *severance*. For a rite of passage to be authentic there must be something we leave behind. Too often, we call something a rite of passage that does not require us to sever from our old way of being. In my own life, I experienced something similar to this when I traveled to Africa, and again when I spent a year traveling around the world, overland across Asia. In a physical way, I was forced to leave something behind in order to become a new person. In traditional cultures, this meant, for example, boys leaving the comfort of the mother, symbolically "severing" the umbilical cord. This could be an extreme and dangerous endeavor that often led to death. Before we judge these cultures for being heartless, we should recall that they had no incidence of teens dying due to drugs and suicide. Moreover, they seldom experience the meaninglessness that afflicts so many in our culture. As Bill Plotkin explains, our society is so concerned with "protecting" our youth, they miss a great deal that rites of passage once provided:

For thousands of years, we have been living in a culture that "protects" us from the hardships and dangers of the descent, a world in which everything is more or less predictable and where most people emulate those getting the most socioeconomic rewards. It is a world from which the true elders have disappeared, the elders who once possessed intimate knowledge of the soul.[6]

I would not, of course, suggest that we risk the lives of our young people. I am proposing not an imitation of traditional rites but new rites based upon traditional principles and some modern values. At some point, either symbolically or physically, the child must experience life away from his comfort zone. At the Chicago Wisdom Project, this has generally meant a retreat in nature.

The second component is *instruction*. Again, this is so often missing from so-called rites of passage in the modern world. In traditional cultures, the initiate learned important skills and myths, gaining entry as a human being in that particular cosmology. I suspect that we have no idea what those capacities might be in our culture. The key is that they are not about getting a job or learning simplistic civics lessons, but about addressing deep questions about what it means to be a human being, about our values. Moreover, regardless of one's job, it is important to have certain capacities. Our young people must learn responsibility, courage, critical thinking, and compassion, not merely job skills. A major part of this process for us has been the students' creative work through which they gain competency in a particular craft.

The third component is *reentry into the community* as a new person. In my own wandering, I did not wish to find some idyllic tropical paradise where I would not have to deal with the aggravations and responsibilities of modern life; my purpose was to return to "the world" as a new person, as a man, ready to transform and teach that world. Our curriculum is designed to expand our students' sense of self and community, to connect them to nature and to issues beyond their daily experience. But we do this in order to allow the students to return to the community in order to transform

[6] Bill Plotkin, *Soulcraft: Crossing into the Mysteries of Nature and Pscyhe* (Novato, CA: New World Library, 2003) p,13-14.

it. So many programs that serve the marginalized focus on "getting out of the ghetto." There is nothing wrong with moving to a safer, cleaner, or more prosperous neighborhood—this is not a judgment against that—but we should remind our youth that they have a responsibility to work for change in their community. Getting a good job does not absolve us of that responsibility. We cannot know that, though, unless we have been taught who we truly are—*we are not our jobs*.

At the Chicago Wisdom Project and at Y.E.L.L.A.W.E. (Youth and Elders Learning Labratory of Ancestral Wisdom Education), we have placed a great deal of emphasis on presenting the creative projects to the community as the culmination of the rite of passage. The students have become teachers. The completion and presentation of the students' creative projects is not the same as the rite of passage, but it is closely linked. This provides the students with an opportunity to celebrate their work and accomplishments. Told they are failures for low test-scores, students can see that they are capable of creating meaningful and powerful work by being authentic and imaginative. Moreover, the students must stand up in front of a group, respond to difficult questions, and be accountable for them selves. This skill—speaking confidently to a group—is as important both for self-esteem and practical purposes as most of what students do in school.

The soul, however one defines it, is as important as any other aspect of the human. We must address our students yearning for meaning, their trauma, and their emotions if we are to truly educate them. Wisdom requires not only that we be able to know the world, but to know our selves as well.

But to truly turn knowledge into wisdom, it must not only pass through the alchemical vessel of the soul; our knowledge must be taken into the world. In short, we must do something. And there is no reason why we should wait until we are in our twenties to do it.

9 DOING

H ow does knowledge become wisdom? One way has to do with how it is applied. That is, knowing a lot of information is useful, but true wisdom comes from the application of those facts to the world. We can say only that we are *knowledgeable* because of what information we know; wisdom comes from the application of knowledge with compassion and insight. Throughout this book I have suggested that our students would benefit from spending less, not more as has frequently been suggested lately, time in school. This chapter is about what else they might be doing, and why.

Some of the activities that take place outside of schools have already been described in other chapters. Students should be spending more time in nature for meditative purposes as well as the rite of passage experience. In this chapter, I will describe another role for nature. Students also should spend time creating art. In this chapter, I will explain the role our students' art can play in society.

This chapter, like so much of this book, requires the reader to simply let go of some of the assumptions we have held—specifically, that most learning happens through books and within classrooms—and reflect on their own experiences. Like me—and I must confess I am pretty intellectual—I suspect that most of us have learned more through experience than through books.

LEARNING BY DOING

When the philosopher John Dewey was running the laboratory school at the University of Chicago nearly a century ago, he based his curriculum on the notion that we learn first and foremost through doing: "Give the pupils something to do, not something to learn; and the doing is of such a nature as to demand thinking; learning naturally results." He advocated such endeavors as cooking food together—not much different from what we are doing in Wisdom Education.

Unfortunately, when I arrived at the University of Chicago in the 90s, his theory of experience (like much of his philosophy) was not being applied in the classroom. Dewey is one of those thinkers whose work is widely read, but has not been integrated into the culture in any meaningful way. Ironically, the philosopher who understood best that learning required an application of ideas into practice is read and discussed in the abstract but not applied. We learn about Dewey's philosophy of education, but we do not educate that way, even in classes that that study it.

For Dewey, learning by doing had to do with a pragmatic concern. He saw that we learn more when we are doing something. Our minds and bodies must work together; we must collaborate and problem-solve with others. Would academia have failed so miserably to recognize the recent economic crisis—or the coming ecological one—had their methods been less abstract and detached from the world? How could so many smart people miss what, in retrospect, seems so obvious? Part of the answer is that they were not doing anything. They spent so much time apart, with their models and formulas, that the messy, chaotic world outside receded into the background as if it were less real.

But there is another reason for action to be part of the curriculum than that the students will learn more. Students can also do something that will transform themselves, their communities, and their world.

COMMUNITY ACTIVISM

I do not believe that education should be limited to seeing that our youth learn more. While this is obviously important, I also believe that our children can begin to work toward making our world more just, sustainable, and compassionate.

I have already argued, for example, that art can play a role in changing our relationship to the world. The fundamental assumptions we make, and our consequent behavior, are shaped not so much by ideas but by myth as conveyed through art. Often, our ideas are merely held because we have taken great pains to conform them to preconceived assumptions and values. We are like Supreme Court justices who claim to be basing decisions on the constitution, but whose judicial skill is primarily an exercise in articulating how to conform the constitution to their values. Creative expression is what shapes those values. With the proper guidance, our young people can create art that shapes their generation. This is no fantasy. Turn on the television and you will find music videos featuring adolescents. The values they espouse and promote are shaped by the corporate executives of the music industry. Why not inspire our youth to create music that expresses different values?

When our students leave the classroom to spend time in nature, there can also be an activist component. The ecosystems of the Earth are dying. Older generations have left the youth with a mass extinction and global warming to deal with. The primary pedagogical and spiritual response to this crisis is to help our children re-embed and reconnect with nature. That is, our youth must transform their relationship to and consciousness of nature. But there is also an activist response to this crisis—and the youth can lead the way. From cleaning our parks to starting recycling programs, young people have already been deeply involved in the so-called "environmentalism" movement. In Wisdom Education, we shift

109

the consciousness from "environment"—background for human civilization—to "ecology" which comes from the Greek word for "home."

For many students, particularly in urban areas, ecology has little appeal. These students have had little connection to nature in their lives. I have worked with students who were nearly adults who still had no idea where their food came from—besides the supermarket or McDonald's. For African American students, environmentalism is often viewed as a white, bourgeois indulgence. The problems of injustice and poverty outweigh problems of nature. This has to do with a resistance to anything connected to rural life after generations of poverty in the South—not to mention the rejection of all things African by the dominant culture—as well as the unfortunate tendency of the environmental movement to fail to see the interconnection of poverty, racism, and ecological destruction.

Our curriculum connects the issues of the students' community with issues that face the world as a whole. Ecology begins with the lack of healthy food in the neighborhood, the prevalence of certain pollution-related diseases among people of color, and the lack of green spaces for the poor. From these issues, the students begin to see how ecology affects them personally. The broader issue of the worldwide crisis then comes alive for them.

With all the justice issues our students discuss, there is an effort made to connect the local and the global. Our Haiti Initiative, for example, was an attempt to empower our youth to help victims of the Haiti earthquake in 2010. But it was also a way for students learn from Haitian culture. African American students began to see the connections between their culture and Haitian culture, between the plight of the Haitian people and their own struggles.

EXPANDING COMMUNITY, EXPANDING SELF

To do something for one's community requires a shift in one's sense of self. We stop seeing ourselves as alone and independent, but as a part of an interdependent web of relationships. Just as ecology teaches us that we are connected to nature, just as the ancestors teach us that the past remains with us, community activism teaches us that we are a part of a community. We depend on the community and it depends on us. The self expands in the process.

Of all the criticism I have levied against Modern education, this is among the most pervasive. Educators send the message to our children that the purpose of school is individual success and achievement. Lip-service is paid to the community, but only to suggest that by becoming individually successful we will be better positioned to help the community. This argument is not entirely false; but it is also somewhat disingenuous. Like the trickle-down theory of economics, this approach to education ignores the reality that many become rich and successful by *increasing* the injustice in our world.

Think of how different the philosophy of Trickle-Down Education is from the ethics of the civil rights movement, in which the individual was asked to risk life and limb for the community. In the process, the world was transformed, not merely in law, but in the consciousness of humanity. It is difficult for any American born after the civil rights movement to comprehend life before it. It is impossible for the participant in the movement not to be transformed.

When we begin to think of ourselves as fundamentally members of community, as relational beings at our core, our identity changes. The answer to the question "Who am I?" changes. I should add that a far more authentic and accurate answer emerges from this process, one that is far more consistent with how humans have lived and defined themselves for most of their history. The idea that we are, at our core, "rugged individualists" is a product of very recent cultural developments that are connected to the basic metaphors and values of Modern education.

Students then move from being individuals, alone in the world, to members of a community. From community issues, students then begin to see that these issues are connected to broader issues. For example, a young person who begins to work for the removal of a dangerous dump in his neighborhood becomes empowered, just as a young person in the civil rights movement would have. And, just as Dr. King connected his people's struggle to the Vietnam War

111

and economic injustice for other marginalized groups, this young person can see how the dump in his neighborhood is connected to economic injustice throughout the United States and toxic dumps found in West Africa where children are poisoned as they scavenge for spare parts.[1] This young person now feels connected to the planet, realizing that the issues affecting him are affecting people all over the world. He no longer is limited to his individual self; his identity has expanded to include the whole planet.

This sort of interconnection is related to but far different from the kind of planetary interconnection we talk about with two very popular and over-emphasized things in educational circles today: globalization and the internet. First, Wisdom Education grounds global interconnection in *felt experience*. The internet connects us superficially while leaving us even more disconnected in meaningful ways. Second, educators, politicians, and bureaucrats cannot seem to stop talking about enabling our youth to "compete in the global economy." The approach in Wisdom Education is not about competition, but about compassion. Good jobs—if they are around—will be found by those who are well educated, not because we create curricula that purport to prepare them for a job we do not even know will exist. Moreover, globalization is based on economic exploitation. Like the internet, it connects superficially—in this case, through consumer products. Those who cannot or will not participate in the global economy are actually *more* disconnected through globalization.

PASSION

At the Chicago Wisdom Project, we have consistently referred to helping students discover their passion. While we have a bias toward art, we do not approach the students by telling them that this is an "arts" program. Some students may not be interested in the traditional arts. The point is not just to inspire students to be "artists"—although that is a good thing—but also to empower them

[1] http://ngm.nationalgeographic.com/2008/01/high-tech-trash/carroll-text

to discover their passion. The "curriculum" then revolves around that passion; the students' work is to go out in the world and do it. Often, of course, this passion is artistic, but it could be anything, really. Our task, as teachers, is not to tell children what they should be interested in, but to provide context for their interests. The learning that occurs and the project-based work the students do with their passion is directed by the teachers and elders so that it can contribute to a more just, sustainable, and compassionate world.

Some passions work better than others, of course. Many students do not know where their passions lie. Others are passionate about television or consumer goods or video games. It takes a lot of work to figure out how some students can do meaningful work when they have spent their lives playing video games and watching television. Part of the work is helping students discover their passions and distinguish between true passions and that which makes them passive consumers.

In one of the classes I teach, a group of young adults in Harvey, Illinois, I decided to ask them what they thought is wrong with the educational system. These students were drop-outs, so I figured they were well positioned to have an opinion on the subject. They came up with a variety of answers, but the one that struck me was a young man who said, "I think we should just let kids pick what they want to do at a young age and let them focus on that. Now, you don't get to do anything you care about until you're grown, and by then you are brain-washed." Exactly.

Another young man said that there was no hope for schools. In high school, there was no way he would go because he cared about nothing but getting high, sex, and money (selling drugs). School was just too boring. I asked him why that was all he cared about. What could schools do differently to make it appealing to someone like him? He thought about it for a moment. "Music," he said. "They could make schools be about music." He thought a little more. "You know, when I was in a school with other people [white and Latino kids] we had music in school all day. And I did better. But when I came out here, to the Black school, we had nothing."

I have been told, in another "Black school" on the south side of Chicago, that it would impossible to have an assembly to raise money for relief for the earthquake in Haiti and to learn about Haitian culture because the test scores were so low that students had to spend all their time preparing for the next test. This kind of backward thinking is the problem. We think that we can tell a child that he should do better in school because one day, decades from now, he will be able to do something he cares about. This just does not work (and, again, there is a subtle racism at play that believes certain kids should not have anything fun or creative because they need to focus on "basic skills"). Schools should be places where students discover their passions and have the opportunity to pursue them. Herein lies the sad irony of our schools: if we would allow are students to do what they love, they would not only be happier: *they would actually learn more and the test scores would go up.*

THE BROADER PURPOSE OF EDUCATION

The role of "doing" in education speaks to the broader purpose of education. If we seek to become educated only for our selves—that is, for our personal wealth and prestige—then we have missed the opportunity for our knowledge to become wisdom. I am proposing that the only way to assess an educational system is to look at the direction in which our communities, our country, our planet, and our species are headed. If the test scores go up but we continue to destroy the Earth, are we succeeding? If we have more graduates, but those graduates or more alienated and their lives continue to be bereft of meaning, are we succeeding? If we have more people prepared for the "global economy" but they lack the critical consciousness to see the transparent lies of our leaders ("Saddam Hussein was responsible for 9-11") are we succeeding? The only assessment that really matters is what our students *do*, not their scores, their jobs, or their degrees.

This speaks to the very definition of wisdom. Part of the way the information we acquire becomes wisdom is by doing something with it. Two people could have the same facts, but do dramatically different things with it. For example, the insights of Einstein could have been used to see our world in a more deeply interconnected way, ushering in an era of creativity that transcends our current worldview; or, it could be used to make atomic bombs. A more just, sustainable, and compassionate world is possible—but it is only possible if we expect our youth to create it. They can do it. They will fear the challenge far less that we do. In fact, they will shine when we call upon them to change their world. In the struggle and in the possibility, they will find their voice and find meaning in a world that, too often, is simply boring.

III *The Movement*

Life is beautiful.
Life is a struggle.
Life is a beautiful struggle.
—Mos Def

THE THIRD AND FINAL SECTION of this book is about practical steps toward transforming education. We have critiqued modern education and proposed some principles around which to organize Wisdom Education. How, then, do we actually make it happen?

The honest answer is that I do not entirely know. The changes I am proposing are radical and will require more than policy or curricular changes. They require changes to our way of thinking about education as well as the structure of schools. And part of this shift in thinking requires us to let go of our tendency to believe learning and child development can be managed in a mechanical way. Dealing with an organic process means dealing with chaos and unpredictability. The movement is unpredictable because it is just that—a movement. The participants—in many cases, this means the youth themselves—will determine its course.

Returning to a couple of important metaphors introduced in section I, imagine that the course of education is like the course of a river. The river is a complex, organic system. We cannot know exactly what the river will look like in a thousand years. If we imagine education is like an automobile, we certainly can know: the automobile will be obsolete and useless. And if we try to control the river, as we so often have, we are likely to render it lifeless.

But there are some practical steps we can take to make this movement grow, and I will share some of what I have learned. This will begin, of course, with the story of my own program in Chicago.

10

THE CHICAGO
WISDOM PROJECT

In the summer of 2009, after having finished graduate school, I packed my little Honda up, along with my wife and one year old daughter, and headed east, back to Chicago. I had been away for six years—four spent in California, two in New York—so, although I had spent my college years and most of my twenties there, I was not sure exactly what to expect.

We camped in the Sierra Nevada Range, near Lake Tahoe, where I saw a bear, then crossed the barren lands of Nevada, nothing but dust and pornography. I have traveled the world, but had never seen anything like the salt flats of Utah that one passes through on the way to Salt Lake City. We recovered for a couple of days there, unsure what to think of the Mormon capital, then moved on to the Rockies. After Colorado, we spent less time in each stop, only really spending any time in Lincoln, Nebraska before finally arriving at our place on the south side of Chicago.

Although the Bay Area as a whole represents one of the world's great urban centers, Chicago felt massive after living in Oakland for four years. There seemed always to be crowds. The air seemed dirtier, the litter more abundant. One could drive all day, it seemed, without getting out of the city, its flat, straight blocks stretching out forever. The city of Chicago seemed to be at war with itself, trying to assert a machine-like efficiency on a chaotic mass of humanity.

I had a bit of money saved, but no job. So, it was in this strange land—one that I thought I knew so well—that I set out to find one.

I had plenty of credentials—advanced degrees, was about to publish a book, had been running an after school program in Oakland—but there really was not a job that I could find that seemed to fit. My credentials, upon further reflection, were better suited for the Bay Area than the Midwest: my degrees were in philosophy and religion from fringe schools; my book was *poetry*; and the after school program I had run was Y.E.L.L.A.W.E.

After half-heartedly applying for a few jobs, I decided that I really did not want to work for someone else. Perhaps my potential employers had perceived this. Finally, I realized what I wanted to do; I realized what Chicago needed.

I met with as many old friends as I could to discuss my ideas about education and how to apply them. Some received my ideas enthusiastically; others were lukewarm. It surprised me, I must admit, that everyone did not leap at the chance to be involved. I figured that those who knew and trusted me would be receptive, of course, but I also thought that people would see that The Chicago Wisdom Project was offering to fill a deep void here. But the truth was that my years away from Chicago had changed me more than I realized, had exposed me to new ways of thinking about things that were difficult to convey to the conservative Midwest.

Nonetheless, I found a small group of supporters. We met and exchanged ideas and contacts. We formed a small board and in September of 2009, founded the Chicago Wisdom Project.

STARTING UP

Although I had worked for many years in the non-profit world, I really had no idea how to start or run one, nor did anyone on our board. Starting a non-profit is relatively simple. First, one must form a board of directors, articles of incorporation, and bylaws. Not really knowing exactly what these were, I went to a bookstore, found a book about doing it, and pretty much used the examples given. Once incorporated, one must then become a 501(c)(3), giving the organization tax-exempt status. This is a bit trickier. For one, the tax forms are more complicated. I elected to use an on-line service to have them filled out to be sure I did it right. I am not sure if this was worth it—our organization had no money and I had to put it all on my credit card—but it probably saved me a lot of time.

One problem with dealing with such matters is that it takes a long time and there is no definitive time frame. Once one fills out the paper work, there is no way to know when the government will give an answer. By November, I had completed the paperwork and simply had to wait.

OBSTACLES

In the meantime, there was work to be done. Chicago presented both advantages and disadvantages to me. The difficulty with working in Chicago was the culture. It is not especially progressive, at least compared to New York or the Bay Area, so many people were not ready for something as radical as I had in mind. Even those who were deeply immersed in working for justice—political radicals—did not seem ready for the paradigm shift I was proposing. The problem lies in the fact that the whole political spectrum is operating out of a similar paradigm. Everyone wants to know what the quantifiable outcomes are.

Without any money in the bank—or even a bank account—I started to try to make some connections. I had worked with youth for many years in Chicago and knew plenty of people. I spoke to a priest in Back-of-the-Yards, a rough neighborhood on the south side, who worked with kids who had been incarcerated. He was interested in what I was doing, but did not really have a group that we could work with regularly. I met with people I had worked with in the past, who generally felt one of two ways: they were either excited and energized by my ideas or stared at me blankly, uncomprehendingly.

In addition to the two old friends who joined my board, it was another old friend who got the Chicago Wisdom Project off the ground. I had known her for years—we had worked for the same organization in Africa—so there was enough trust for her to give me a chance. This, I found, was one of the biggest obstacles we faced in starting something new and radical: most people are not willing to trust you if they don't know you. In Chicago, I would find, this was part of a vicious circle of corruption and dishonesty. At every turn, I encountered people who said they wanted to help but had other motives.

"Roger," for example, said he wanted to mentor with us. During the course of our interview, it came out that he wanted to get some fundraising experience. He offered to learn on the job as our fundraiser. Since we had no fundraiser and no money to hire one, this seemed like a good move for us. And it was. "Roger" managed to raise some money for us—all from a wealthy friend. But as soon as I provided him with a reference, he vanished.

The most dramatic example came when we held our first fundraiser. This was to get us off the ground, to get a little bit of money to open a bank account and get things started. We had no idea what we were doing. Most venues are prohibitively expensive—well over $2,000, an amount that we were not even sure we could gross. But a couple of musician friends recommended a place called "Quennect Four," an underground venue that had the radical, revolutionary philosophy we were looking for. There were revolutionary slogans on the walls. "John," the guy who ran the place, offered to let us hold the event for free. "We just want to help," he told us. But it soon became apparent that fundraisers at this venue were meant to fund other activities as well. John had a chronic case of the sniffles, and he seemed to sleep all day. After our event John started calling and texting me, saying I had left and he had to "pay for everything himself." I had given his girlfriend the $250 that we had agreed upon, but she claimed not to remember how much I had given her. He was clearly angry that we had taken off with the money we had taken in. I learned the hard way that sometimes "revolution" is a hustle, more about the *scene* than the movement.

YOUTHBUILD

We made a little bit of money, enough to open a bank account and cover some expenses. We had already started working with our first group, in the YouthBuild program in Harvey. Harvey is a suburb south of Chicago. It has little in common with what most of us think of as suburban life. In recent years, as wealth has returned to the city and urban neighborhoods have gentrified, much of the poverty of Chicago has moved to the periphery, to places like Harvey. All the violence, drugs and problems that would be found in an urban housing project could be found in Harvey, but with even less access to resources.

My task was to apply the Chicago Wisdom Project curriculum to a group of 18 to 24 year olds who had dropped out of school and were pursuing a GED and learning some building skills. In some ways, this was an ideal group. When I introduce a subversive idea, something that challenges what it taught in school, I never have a problem getting these young people on board. The system has not worked for them. They are dropouts; many have been incarcerated. They have little trust in anyone, particularly the system.

The Chicago Wisdom Project works well with this group for another reason. They are taking GED classes and getting job training to get some of the basic skills they need. But this does not mean that they do not have the intellectual capacity to discuss deeper, more complex, and more interesting topics than what they get in their GED class. My classes were like college classes, and they appreciated that fact.

Finally, they appreciated the opportunity for creative expression. There were some extremely talented young people in the class. My class allowed them to do what they were already good at, not focus on their failings.

That is not to say that this group was easy to work with or without struggles. There were many things about my application of the curriculum and the details of the partnership that I had to work through as we went along.

SPRINGTIME
OUR MODEL GROUP

The winter months in Chicago—my first real winter in four years—bore down on me. The grayness of each day faded mercilessly into each long night. I waited for funding opportunities that were scarce and for the mysterious letter from the IRS to arrive. The economic situation at large was bleak—in the midst of the most severe financial crisis of my lifetime, fundraising was extremely difficult. Without our 501(c)(3), I tried to find wealthy donors. I reached out to people from my past, but few gave me a dime. I was struggling emotionally and the financial situation of the Chicago Wisdom Project was taking its toll on my family.

During that first winter, we decided to start another group. Several attempts at alternative partnerships had fallen through, and we decided that it would be useful to work with a group of students without any partner. As helpful as it was to work with YouthBuild, there were limitations to what we could do with them. If we could select a group of students to have our own program—the first time this would have happened anywhere, including California where we partnered with a school—this would allow for our complete vision to unfold. Things that are difficult in other contexts—the rite of passage ceremony, for example—could be enacted.

We found a group of kids that we knew. Some were the children of friends; many came from the Sue Duncan Children's Center. Things had come full circle for me. I was working with the younger brothers and sisters of those I had worked with years ago. I knew most of the parents and they trusted me. Some of the kids I had known since they were born. This program has evolved into a full partnership with the Sue Duncan Children's Center. At the time of writing, The Chicago Wisdom Project was in charge of the group activities for the middle school students at the Sue Duncan Children's Center.

THE RETREAT

When YouthBuild ended in June, we focused on our first retreat with the new group. We took them to a place in nearby Michigan where we could share a large cabin with multiple rooms. From everyone's perspective, the retreat was a great success. The students felt it was the highlight of their experience; the teachers considered it a transformative experience. We learned how to make a fire and about edible and poisonous plants; we had a ritual in which the students considered, in silence and in the woods, what they would like to leave behind; and, of course, there was the midnight walk to look at the stars. Just as important was a late night prank the girls played on the boys—these kinds of things are important memories for our kids.

The retreat, like the new group as a whole, was an opportunity for us to learn about what a longer retreat might look like and how to go about making it happen. This was a shorter, preliminary retreat. This group will have a longer, more in depth experience in the spring.

In addition, this was an opportunity to build the cohesiveness of the group. An essential part of Wisdom Education is the collaboration that takes place. Students not only collaborate in their creative work, but also in supporting one another. They learn to discuss meaningful issues in a compassionate way. While debate is an emphasis in many schools, it is usually—in, for example, debate clubs—for the sport of defeating an adversary. Our students learn to listen to one another, because each group is like a family.

THE SCHOOL
CHAOS AND RIGIDITY

I spent the rest of the summer working on an updated curriculum, which can be found in the appendix. I also began to work on some new partnerships. The worst of those partnerships was with a school. Nothing about the atmosphere of the school suited our work. We could not even meditate because there were so many interruptions. Students missed class because of detention.

The best way to describe the problem with the partnership, however (aside from the things like the fact that we were never paid on time) was that there was not an atmosphere conducive to transformation. The school wavered between chaotic and regimented, but it was never peaceful, creative, or nurturing. Of course, there were individuals in the school who brought these qualities, but it was not part of the culture of the institution.

And there was a sort of unspoken competition for the students. We were the losers, because we had only six regular attendees. Other classes, which had titles (like "cheerleading") much more easily grasped, were more popular. Had we done an ice-cream sundae making class we would have been very successful, in their eyes. The truth was that they had no vision for their after-school program. It was all about the numbers.

THE LEARNING LABORATORY

Another partnership seemed to fit better with our project. A friend of mine, after graduating from the University of Chicago's divinity school, became the pastor of a south side church with a long time interest in the arts and activism. He gave us the space to create a "learning laboratory"[1]—a place where youth could freely explore their imagination and express their creativity.

For example, we received a small grant to build a recording studio. A large number of our students, especially in YouthBuild, were interested in music. The students rebuilt the room from scratch, cleaning, painting, and setting up the recording studio. At the time of writing, they are beginning to record their own music, music that can counter the images and messages that dominate the mainstream. We have two pottery wheels for the students to work with. Additionally, students use this space to work on their writing. We have published one collection of poetry and have more students ready to publish books.

THE NATIONWIDE MOVEMENT

We are only planters. Our experiences have given us the ability to put seeds in the ground, but nothing more. Each community must cultivate its own Wisdom Education, its own children.

---

[1] I have borrowed this term from Matthew Fox

Rather than grow the Chicago Wisdom Project to become a huge institution that will be run mechanically rather than respond organically to our rapidly changing world, we will continue to work with our partners on a small scale as a way to influence the educational landscape. In time, new sites will arise—each different depending on the needs of a given community—until, ultimately, wisdom schools are born.

In addition to Chicago and Oakland, we are working to begin program at several sites around the country at the time of writing. We are building our own location for retreats and summer camps on a 16-acre permaculture farm in Michigan. The advantage of being widespread is that we can see new possibilities for Wisdom Education from each individual program (or school). Ultimately, we envision a *Global* Wisdom Project, a network of programs that seek to educe the wisdom of peoples all over the planet.

At the time of writing—the end of our third year—we have finally reached the point of being able to pay our teachers and to pay rent in our own space and are working with stable partners throughout the south side of Chicago. We conduct Wisdom Teacher training programs to train teachers nationwide. Wisdom cannot come from one individual or institution; it must arise in dialogue.

127

11 JOINING THE MOVEMENT

CHAPTER

The Chicago Wisdom Project is only one manifestation of Wisdom Education. I have little interest in growing the Chicago Wisdom Project into a massive institution; rather, I am hoping that others will start their own wisdom projects, that schools and parents will seek to educate our children based upon the principles of Wisdom Education. This means that I have as much interest in drawing others into the movement as in the success of the Chicago Wisdom Project. Of course I want it to succeed—which means, unfortunately, raising money consistently—but in the end it matters little if the movement is advanced by the Chicago Wisdom Project or by some other entity.

While not exactly a how-to guide, this chapter provides some advice on how to join the movement and to start one's own program. The appendices provide additional content, such as a curriculum and contact information. It is my hope that the movement is not limited by my own thoughts and ideas, but that whatever I present here can be a starting point on which to expand.

THE NEED FOR A MOVEMENT

We are at a turning point. Things must change quickly and peacefully or they will certainly change rapidly and violently. There are various ways to think about change, and all are important. For example, activists consistently have fought against political and economic injustice through direct confrontation. In the political realm, change happens through the passage of laws and decisions made regarding how money is spent by the government. If activists are organized enough and politicians are radical enough, *systemic* change can come about. That is, we can do more than just put bandages on the gaping wounds of our society. Systemic change transforms society.

But how do we get activists, politicians and others to recognize the need for systemic change? One challenge we face as a civilization—and every civilization at a crisis point faces—is that changing the mindset, the worldview, the consciousness of the people is very difficult to do because we educate our children based upon the values of the old paradigm. The obvious solution lies in our educational systems. That is, if we want the next generation to reimagine our world, we must educate them differently. The problem here lies in the fact that to do so requires systemic change. We are trapped in a vicious circle.

It would be naïve to think that politicians will decide to change their approach to education. The best we can hope for from them is that they will at least provide better funding for the same old failing ideas.

We can, however, begin to change people's minds. It is not easy, but it is possible. And it is work that cannot be done merely by presenting ideas. It requires us to engage in the very work that Wisdom Education promotes. That is, we must tell better stories, use better metaphors, and convey better values. This requires us to put our philosophy in action. Talking and writing are not enough. The ideas presented here—or on a blog or in a classroom—must enter into the laboratory in which the student and the teacher, the child and the elder, engage the work of bringing forth wisdom.

It is my feeling that this is best done through a movement, not an institution. Institutions are, of course, easier to control than movements. And we need them, too. Without any institutional support it would be very unlikely that we would reach a large number of students. There are already institutions that are dedicated to the movement. In addition to these, there are other like-minded (or at least open-minded) institutions with whom we have partnered.

But the movement is something more than these institutions. The movement happens when a group of kids are on the corner. It happens when people meet in coffee houses and in basements. It happens when we write poems or music—when we are not even thinking about education or the movement at all. A movement can, and should, involve those who have nothing to do with education other than the fact that we all have something to learn and something to teach.

By thinking in terms of a movement, we are freed from the constraints of what we can organize by our selves and of how much money we can raise. Anyone can join the movement: people who work in schools, martial arts teachers, artists, administrators, teachers, counselors, college professors, philanthropists.

JOIN THE MOVEMENT

Most books are read, placed neatly back on the shelf, and, while perhaps not completely forgotten, do little to change one's behavior. A great book, however, shifts one's consciousness in subtle ways. Our behavior changes not because we seek to do anything different, but because we begin to look at the world differently. We change and our actions subsequently change.

This is not a great book, but a manifesto. It is a call to do something. I am asking the reader not to put the book back on the shelf hoping that perhaps some deep, interior process will lead to a more fundamental change in behavior; I am asking the reader to join the movement.

SCHOOLS

For the sake of transparency, I should make a confession: I do not like schools. That is not exactly true. I like the graduate schools I attended. My daughter's school—a Montessori school—is great.

And I am sure that there are many schools throughout the country that I would love. Most of them are small and private, I suspect. While no one would exactly say it this way, we have made a decision as a society that certain kinds of schools are appropriate for the rich (open and nurturing) and others for the poor (rigid and institutional).

Public schools, for those who have not been in one lately, are generally awful places. The kids are micromanaged throughout the day. They are constantly tested and assessed. They seldom have free play and even less frequently go outside. The food is highly processed—interestingly, from the same sources as *prison food*. The teachers and administrators are overworked, under pressure, and generally in a bad mood.

Charter schools can be pretty much put in the same category. While the ideal behind them is often noble and novel, they are forced to adhere to the same standards as public schools. Under pressure to have high test scores in order to have their charter renewed, the idealism on which they were founded us often lost. And many charter schools were not founded on such ideals, in spite of the way politicians have portrayed them: in fact, many charter schools are run by for-profit corporations; their only interest is in high test scores to get the charter renewed and to keep the money coming in.

Many will object to this admittedly subjective and over-generalized portrait of schools. I would simply ask the reader to go to any large public school where many poor children go and take a look to judge for your self. For every teacher who disagrees with me, I can find ten who have quit or want to quit teaching for the reasons I give.

So why can we not have a wisdom school for everyone? What would it look like? The greatest challenge is exactly what charter schools have confronted. In order to retain a charter, so many compromises are often made that the school ends up looking a lot like every other school. How can we confront the tyranny of conformity? The answer, I believe, is not to compromise but to remain true to our principles.

There are simply schools and school systems that will never be open to such an approach. In these cases, there are still ways to implement a Wisdom Education program. For example, we have taught classes and run after-school programs in schools. Again, one must still be careful: if the school is not a good fit, it will be extremely difficult to truly implement the program. At the time of writing, we are working as a subversive force, at the margins of the school system.

In time, however, I believe that there will be an increased desire for Wisdom Education in districts around the country. As the school system continues to fail—and it will—people will be increasingly interested in innovation. At this time, "innovation"—see the "race to the top"—usually refers to not-particularly-innovative ways to teach to the test. But there will be districts in which desperation finally opens up possibilities. When we see that high test scores do not mean much for a nation in decline, and that even teaching to the test does not do much for the test scores anyway, Wisdom Schools will become a reality.

Ultimately, for Wisdom Education to truly take root, I believe Wisdom Schools are a necessity. If one problem with schools is that anything "extra-curricular" is, by definition, marginalized, then it is essential to educate our children holistically, with a wisdom-based curriculum that integrates all the elements of Wisdom Education. These should not be "subjects" but elements woven into every aspect of school. This includes both pedagogical categories—embodied practice, soul work, intellectual content, and creative expression—and curricular design. By curricular design I refer to the way in which a school day, a school year, and an entire school is shaped by content.

The content of the wisdom school should be shaped by story rather than information. What, we might ask, is the story that connects us to one another while honoring our individuality? That can teach us our place in the world and give us the wisdom—not merely the skills, for without wisdom we cannot know which skills we need or how to use them—to navigate the 21st century? The story cannot and should not be the same for every school, but I would suggest that it should be interdisciplinary, combining artistic and scientific insights.

For example, we might design a high school curriculum that begins and ends with the question, "Who am I?" To answer such a question, we would have to explore science through ecology, the body, and the Universe Story as a starting point. Students would need to understand mathematics to understand these stories; and they could learn them through cooking and gardening, through observing the heavens, and through spending time in nature.

But scientific approaches would not tell the whole story. Students would learn the history of ideas as well, starting with creation myths and evolving into more complex philosophical and religious concepts as they got older. They would explore poetry, visual arts, and fiction.

The reader will notice that we have already addressed most of the elements of Wisdom Education: Studying literature and science requires the intellect; studying science involves the body and nature; studying myth and literature and art requires creativity and imagination; and woven throughout all these studies is "doing." The ultimate test of a student's learning would be in their capacity to express themselves creatively, innovatively, and collaboratively. A great deal has already been said about the value of students' creative projects, but I would like to add something about the value of original ideas. Even when students are not engaging in "the arts" they can be creative. The youth can and should learn to write well, to express original ideas clearly and succinctly. They should learn to express themselves in front of a group, too. Finally, there is no reason to discourage collaboration. Students will learn more from collaborative projects than from studying for tests. As Sir Ken Robinson says, what the rest of the world calls collaboration, schools call "cheating."[1]

In addition to the curricular structure, wisdom schools should weave the various pedagogical elements throughout the school day. Since there are no "subjects," the school must integrate these

---

[1] http://www.youtube.com/watch?v=zDZFcDGpL4U

elements. A starting point is for a teacher to ask the following before a discussion or project is begun:

ᴥ *Embodied Practice*: How can the students involve their bodies in this process? In what ways can we use non-verbal, meditative practices to augment the learning?

ᴥ *Soul Work*: How is this giving the students (and the teacher) a deeper sense of meaning in their lives? How can this experience be healing as well as informative?

ᴥ *Intellectual Content*: What are the values conveyed by the content of this discussion? Are the students learning to ask deep questions and to become critically conscious?

ᴥ *Creative Expression*: How can the students express themselves in response to this work?

There are times, of course, when some of the above pedagogical categories will exist without direct reference to the curriculum. For example, students sometimes need to do some soul work that has nothing to do with ideas. Sometimes, they need some therapy apart from the curriculum. And that is OK. The point is not to *deny* soul work to those students not apparently in crisis—after all, we are all part of a *civilization* in crisis.

While we are breaking down the curricular and pedagogical barriers, we may as well break down a third barrier in our schools—age and grade level. It is, of course, appropriate for some instruction to occur based on a child's age, but there is no reason not to integrate children of different ages. Students learn a great deal from teaching their younger peers, and young children often respond best to other kids. Perhaps more radical is generational integration. We must figure out a way to include not only parents, but also elders in our schools.

THE ROLE OF PARENTS AND ELDERS

As a parent, I want to know what I can do now for my daughter in the absence of a Wisdom School. How can we raise our sons and

135

daughters to be real men and women—*warriors* who have a sense of who they are, who take responsibility for them selves, and have the courage to confront our challenges with integrity—when our school system fails to address this need? Given that most parents will not be able to change the school system—at least not over-night—what can parents do? As it turns out, quite a lot.

If the bad news is that parents cannot get the schools to raise children as they would like, the good news is that parents are still the most important people in a child's life. Far more than anything that happens in school, parents determine a child's success or fail-ure in school. I went to an elite college because of the way my par-ents raised me, not because of the (rather mediocre) academics at my high school. There are, of course, some things parents cannot do. Our children are in school for so many hours and its influence on our children is so great. But because of this fact, parents have let go of some of the responsibilities that should always have been theirs.

For example, every community can create authentic rites of pas-sage. For any school to take over this role—as most schools are currently constructed—would require radical change. When an eighth grade graduation represents a child's only coming of age ceremony, the child has been deprived. A school-based rite of pas-sage, in the absence of Wisdom Schools, is invariably watered-down.

Fundamentally, wisdom has to do not only with content, but also, and more importantly, with creating an atmosphere where learning is sacred. Schools must do this; but anyone who has been in the sterile environment of most schools knows this is unlikely. A parent can do this far more easily. This means not only turning off the television, but also not revolving the home life around it. How many homes focus on the television, as if it were the hearth or the altar? How many homes have a television in every room? If only television were the only medium that distracted our children from other people, from nature, from *themselves*. Parents have a respon-sibility to keep the cell phones, the video games, and the internet in the background. And much of it is altogether unnecessary for children. The oft-heard argument that children have cell phone for safety is disingenuous at best—children have cell phone because parents are living in fear and are afraid to say no. Creating an atmosphere in which conversation, music, and books are central will go a long way. We can also simply take our children outside more nd encourage them to be in nature and play freely and imaginatively. This can be challenging for parents who have little free time of their own or who do not live near safe, clean, green spaces. In addition, schools have so little trust in parents that they often give absurd amounts of homework to children. Many grade school aged children today have several hours of homework a night. Parents must challenge school on this and many other issues.

All of these changes, because they run counter to the prevailing cultural currents, seem difficult. But parents must have the courage to choose to adopt different values for their children.

Finally, for a learning community to take shape requires the participation of the elders. For too long, our elders have been marginalized. Perhaps they suffer more than any other age group from the generational fragmentation of our society. Placed in nursing homes and largely ignored, the wisdom of the elders is absent in a culture that favors progress over history. While any educational program quite obviously focuses on the youth, a special role for the elders will enrich the experience for all generations. Young teachers, parents, and mentors need the guidance of elders just as much as students.

THE ROLE OF THE YOUTH

For too long, we have talked about how to improve our children's educational experiences, to enhance the world for which they will become responsible, without involving them in the process. If Wisdom Education recognizes the need to honor the wisdom of the ancestors, the elders, and traditional ways of knowing, it places just as much faith in the youth for their inherent wisdom, creativity, and subversive energy. There is no generation alive in the United States today, no matter how old, which has not thoroughly messed things up. Why not put some responsibility on the youth? It is, after all, the youth who will have to deal with the mistakes of the older generations.

The challenge for the youth begins with turning off the gadgets. I recognize that technology *per se* is not bad. People will use it, as I do, and there is nothing wrong with doing so. But there is a way to put technology to good use and a way to use it for self-destruction, -pacification, or -distraction. I can feel the generation gap between myself and today's teenagers most profoundly when they are dealing with phones or Facebook. They know no other world. They cannot imagine not communicating via text messages. This generation is the most easily-controlled in history. They do not think, do not have time for quiet. My challenge to them is simple: Since your parents will not make you do it, do you have the courage to stop talking on the phone, to stop texting, and to face the (admittedly scary) world?

As an alternative, the youth must be truly creative. Do not wait for an invitation from adults to express your selves. There are opportunities all around. Youth do have access to more creative media than ever before. The challenge is to stop being passive consumers and to become creators. On a basic level, this requires our youth simply to tell their stories. The greatest gift they can give to themselves and to the world is to tell their stories.

To do any of this, we require the youth to challenge the paradigm that so profoundly limits them. Far too often, young people think they are challenging the adults around them, think they are being rebellious, when all they are doing is falling into the trap of mindless consumerism. I am calling on the youth of today to challenge us—not by being disrespectful, but by truly challenging the values of the world we have created for you.

Think of this chapter as an invitation. While I talked a great deal about schools, there is still much work to be done for the Wisdom School to take shape. Many blanks need to be filled in. And this is how it should be. Draw from the resources and ideas presented here and use your own imagination to bring something new forth.

12 WISDOM EDUCATION, WISDOM CIVILIZATION

The work of education, of course, is not to make better schools, but to make a better world. Too often, I believe, educators forget this obvious and simple truth. Discussions about education seldom reflect the kind of world we might imagine is possible; rather, they focus on achievement and success within a given paradigm. Educators seem not to realize that the way we educate our children creates, reinforces, or shatters the paradigm.

For example, when we assume that the purpose of education is to help students find a job in the global economy, we forget that the "global economy" is not some force of nature. Humans created it. It exists because of the decisions we made, decisions based upon how we view the world, which is based on the way we have been educated.

While what goes on in a school is important in itself—after all, our children spend most of their childhoods there—the ultimate relevance of a school is what kind of civilization it inspires our children to create. A school is not "good" if its students get good test scores but are so unhappy, so disconnected, and so unable to think critically that they go out in the world and commit acts of violence and destruction. Such schools only give more power to the mis-educated, who become what Wendell Berry calls "itinerant professional vandals." I think I prefer the "bad" schools.

Modern industrial culture is ill equipped to deal with the crises of this moment. For the first time in human history, we face a mass-extinction that threatens the viability of life on the planet. This crisis was largely created by modern industrial culture. Its values can only lead to more destruction.

In this final chapter, therefore, I would like to give some attention to what I believe to be the real consequences—good and bad—of the choices we make about how we educate our children. On the one hand, we have the current model in which the world is the marketplace for global capitalism, the school a factory, and the child a machine; on the other hand . . . this is a hand is empty, a story we have not yet told. In part, it is our responsibility to offer our children a new vision. But we also must empower our children to become mythmakers, to tell the story of their generation themselves.

WHAT'S AT STAKE

I have argued throughout this book that the metaphors, narratives, and values of our educational system are problematic. This can be argued strictly on an educational level. That is, we can show how the current educational system simply does not work. Our children are becoming less, not more, educated through it. I would like to leave that argument behind now, and address what I think is at the core of the need for a Wisdom Education Movement. That is, even if the Modern educational system did work within its own artificial and self-serving parameters—it is telling, I think, that educators have so much trouble showing this considering how easy it generally is to invent criteria that validates a given system—it will fail in the consequences it has for the planet and for our species. This is at the heart of our reason for educating children in the first place. Seldom, if ever, do educators discuss it. They may argue that this is because it cannot be proven quantifiably. If they do, they will have proven my point.

So what are the consequences of our current educational system? First, our school system, in using mechanistic metaphors, raises children to relate to the world as a machine. The consequences of this are clear and devastating. We can talk about "greening" our schools and tell our youth to recycle all we want, but if we continue to instill in them the notion that the world is a machine, they will unthinkingly relate to it as a resource to be used and manipulated. They will not value it.

The consequences of not valuing the Earth, of not holding it sacred, are expressed largely through the system of global, industrial capitalism. The criticism here is not with the notion of "free-enterprise," but with the notion that the economy is primary, ecology secondary. Economics dominates nearly every aspect of the public discourse, including education. In fact, economics, in its proper place, refers to the way we use and exchange resources. It is a subset of ecology. To be a human being, to survive, requires first to be embedded in a web of life. Without our primary relationship being to ecology, we behave as though we are disconnected from the Earth. When we consider the economy to be primary, we make choices—not simply individual ones, but civilizational choices—that express this devaluing of the Earth.[1]

A myth is most fundamentally about how we understand our place in the world. In the Myth of Modernity, we believe it is our place to manage, subdue, and control the Earth through the mechanisms of global, industrial capitalism. The only answers we can come up within this paradigm continue to reinforce this skewed relation. We believe that capitalism and technology, for example, are the solution to the ecological crisis.

While technology can and should be part of the solution, we cannot solve our problems through the same mentality that created them. Technological and capitalistic solutions are popular with politicians for one simple reason: *these solutions do not require a change in mentality or lifestyle on the part of wealthy, Western nations.* The reality of the situation is quite different. As resources are depleted, as pollution and global warming intensify, and as species

---

[1] See Thomas Berry, *The Dream of the Earth* (Sierra Club Books, 2006)

become extinct, we are faced with a choice if we are to survive: *either wealthy nations dramatically reduce consumption or we force— and increasingly, this force will truly be enforced by force—the world's poor to continue to live in squalor.* We cannot sustain our current consumption patterns, particularly if the world's poor demand an increasingly large piece of the pie.

What's at stake, therefore, is our survival. The Myth of Modernity, reinforced in our educational systems, perpetuates a worldview that not only encourages us to act as we do; it does not allow us to act any other way. Personal discipline or lack of information is not the problem. The problem is that we have been trained by our schools to see the world in a particular way. And this is leading to our demise.

Metaphors, if they are powerful enough, have a way of becoming real no matter how absurd they are. Our schools have painted a picture of the world for our students in three ways that I believe are shaping the world for them.

(1) World as Factory. The view of the world as a factory begins with our schools. As parents have been required to work long hours to support the economy, the school has arisen as a sort of warehouse for children. As much as politicians and educators talk about reducing class size, the reality is that the very existence of the school in its current form is owed in part to the need to have as many children tended by as few adults as possible. If this were not the case, parents would be home with their children for many more hours than they are.

The design of the school—particularly the modern high school—is modeled on the assembly line of the factory. This was done for optimal efficiency and to best acclimate students to factory work when they were finished with high school. Only a select few were supposed to go on to college. For example, in my hometown, Rochester, NY, most of those who graduated from high school when my high school was built would have worked for Kodak. Most of the men of my father's generation worked there.

Although there are few factory jobs available for high school graduates today, the same basic model exists. The metaphor is expressed in the very structure of the school. If we began with an organic metaphor, we would give birth to nurturing spaces for education, but the modern school, like the factory, is designed for efficiency. And the minds of the students who have gone through such a school have been shaped to view the world through this lens. The school, after all, is a small world, a microcosm. It provides a paradigm for an individual to shape the broader world.

This metaphor of the school as a factory leads not only to viewing the world as a factory, but also to viewing the human as a machine. The mechanistic approach to life is expressed in our attitude toward the Earth, in our unwavering belief that technology alone can solve the ecological crisis. Moreover, it leads to an impoverishment in the way we experience life. We attempt to pave over and mechanize that which is free and unpredictable. Indeed, our notion of freedom has been skewed to the point that we equate freedom with the freedom to do business and to shop.

(2) World as Prison. This metaphor has two consequences that are related but have profoundly different consequences. Many of our schools provide a direct pipeline for certain populations of students to go to prison. So much time, money, and energy is spent on punishing the youth that they have learned, much more than any information on the curriculum, that they are profoundly damaged and insufficient. They are ready for prison.

I suggest that the reader visits an "inner city" school (again, this is the code word for a school attended mostly by black or brown children). You will find a remarkable amount of energy spent on managing and disciplining the students. There will be complex codes that manage everything from the way they walk down the hall to how they sit in their chair. You will also find a few individuals whose job, as far as I can tell, is screaming at the students. William Ayers writes that "zero tolerance policies" lead to a climate in which:

[c]riminal justice metaphors and practices are embraced, and the great humanizing mission of education is lost. These policies are a cultural and political attack on the idea of inclusive, demo-

143

cratic schooling. Classrooms become sterile and one-dimensional places devoid of teachable moments: Every misbehavior warrants a trip to the office, teacher judgment and wisdom are curtailed, and schools become narrower, narrower, narrower, until they are nothing more than little training prisons.[2]

While clearly such schools and such a system represent an implicit racism and classism in our society, I would suggest that this is only an extreme manifestation of a deeper message conveyed to all students: *School is not a place of joy and exploration, but something to escape.* This notion is deeply rooted in a cultural bias that, along with the dualism of mind and body described in chapter 7, understands our world as something flawed and insufficient, something to escape, not to cherish.

(3) World as mall. This worldview is not exactly expressed in the structure of the school, but in the values that are conveyed to our children in terms of aspiration. The American dream is based on the notion that if we work hard enough, we can escape the factory and the prison. The problem with this myth is that we have conveyed to our youth, through our schools, a vision of the world as a factory or a prison. Fundamentalist religion is so appealing in the United States in large part for this reason. Rejecting the consumerist values, the fundamentalist realizes that the great hope lies beyond. Injustice in the world does not matter, ecological destruction does not matter, because nature and humanity are irredeemable.

The other side of the same coin is the consumerist, who sees the world as a mall. It is not joyous, but it can be enjoyed if we have the money to buy enough of it. Because schools basically present our students with an image of the world as factory or prison, the only hope they can offer is the American dream. Each child believes that, while most will end up in the factories (the working classes) or in prison (the underclasses), he will become rich.

To find value in such a world, a person must, like their political

---

[2] William Ayers, *Teaching Toward Freedom*, p. 25

ally, the fundamentalist, give all his power to the corporation. Injustice and the ecological collapse are ignored because they would require the individual to take responsibility for his actions. Thanks to a lack of rites of passage in our culture, we are not overwhelmed with people willing to take responsibility for their actions.

Enjoyment in such a world—for there is little joy—is found in the fleeting pleasures of meaningless consumption—the latest cell phone, the new car, etc. We become increasingly obese, watch television ostensibly to amuse ourselves but really to find out what to buy.

The human, in such a world, is defined not by an organic process, but by the resume—two-dimensional, frozen in time, and without the possibility for dialogue. Because the human has no inherent value, we try to buy and achieve our way to value. We are a list of accomplishments and possessions. The disembodied Facebook page is more real to us than our bodies.

This is the world we are making through our schools. If the American Dream is the core myth of our schools, it has given our children an image of the world as a factory in which we take resources without compassion and foresight; a prison from which we only want to escape; and a mall from which value is derived only through buying. The human, according to this myth, is a mere machine, her core identity found on a Facebook page or resume.

Look around. This is not a prediction, but an observation. This is the world we have made. Fortunately, we are not machines, or resumes, or consumers. We have the capacity to create a new world. To do so, we will have to educate our children in a radically different way.

BECOMING MYTHMAKERS

To subvert this paradigm, to create a new narrative for our civilization, we must transform our way of looking at the world. This is an educational issue. Western civilization has been built with knowledge. An educational approach that emphasized abstract knowledge has enabled us to manipulate our world in remarkable ways. In the form of ecological destruction and a culture of meaninglessness and alienation, we have reached the end of this paradigm. This book has been about Wisdom Education. What does the world we create from this educational paradigm look like?

No one can precisely say what a contemporary wisdom civilization would look like. We have examples from the past and can imagine the future, but there is no contemporary example. Rather than thinking of what outcomes we want, I believe it is best to focus on that which is most meaningful in the present. In the case of a school, this means creating a nurturing, creative, joyous, inspiring place. The specifics of what comes forth will be uncertain, but it will certainly be better than what we have now. We cannot know the outcomes we seek; for in an organic process, those outcomes are partly determined in the process.

I am arguing for no specific outcomes in education. Rather, I am suggesting that if we can inspire our youth to create the right myths, we can give birth to a wisdom civilization. This means we must educate our children holistically, connecting their psyche and the world at large; connecting their bodies and their minds; connecting theory and action; and tying it all together through their creative expression.

While our youth can and will create these myths, they need and want guidance. We can offer some values and some metaphors from which to proceed. While we cannot tell another's story, we can suggest what we might want to learn from that story. For example, if I hear a song on the radio that glorifies crass-consumerism, violence and misogyny, I can criticize it. The oft-heard defense that "this is my experience" is a cowardly cop-out, a failure to confront the demons of our culture, consumerism and violence. That same experience can and should be told. We need to hear the stories of violence in our communities. But we do not have to glorify the violence.

The youth are not to blame. They have not experienced rites of passage to help them become men and women. It is the responsibility of the older generation to make sure they do. And when they do, they will have the strength to truly confront their demons, not to submit meekly to them.

It is my hope that the stories told by the next generation, my daughter's generation, will be stories of integration and connection rather than of alienation and individualism. That is not to say that the experience of isolation is not something to be addressed. Humanity is enduring a profound transition. This, the story of our lostness, must be told. But it must be told in order to overcome it, not to reinforce the values of "rugged independence."

From the creative expression of our interconnection, we can begin to be more compassionate. We are connected not only internally—mind, body, and soul—but with one another. We are connected temporally to our ancestors, who in turn connect us to the entire world.

The work of the mythmaker is to tell us who we are. Just as the myths of the Modern school tells us we are machines or prisoners or consumers, a new myth can tell us something else entirely. Ultimately, this identity can reveal that we are really not that different, not that separate from one another. Your suffering is mine; the destruction of a forest is the destruction of a part of me.

Dr. King believed that "unmerited suffering is redemptive" because his worldview was based upon the notion of the "Beloved Community," an interconnected web of relationships that defines us. Our redemption is found not in some abstract doctrine about the suffering of a man millennia ago, but of the insight that our own suffering allows us to have compassion for another's. We are redeemed—that is, we awaken to truly know who we are—when we recognize that our authentic identity is found in relationship. In a culture which values independence over interdependence—just as King discovered it valued segregation over integration—we cannot be saved by conformity. Education must be subversive.

Human salvation lies in the hands of the creatively maladjusted.

MY DAUGHTER'S FUTURE

epilogue

Thirty years from now—give or take a few years—I see my daughter as a new parent, as I am now. My hope is that parenthood is as thrilling for her as it is for me, that she will cherish the opportunity to spend time with her child and won't be too busy checking email and making money.

My dream is that she will grow up in a world in which the possibility of raising a child is not limited by ecological collapse, by inequities that consign the masses to poverty and despair. Equally important is that she grows up in a culture where she can raise a child in a world where parenting has become such a lost art—how often do we consider that parenting is, in fact, an art?—that our focus is pacification over exploration, management over empowerment, fear over love.

My dream is that one day, she will take walks with her child, as I once did with her. That she will even find the green space to do so, that the air will be clean enough to want to breath, that there will be birds and trees to stir the senses, is no given.

Dreams are not about certitude. By their very nature, they require us both to imagine that which we fear may not exist as well as that which has never existed before.

I do not expect that all of our ecological, political, and economic problems will go away. Even if—even when—we recreate our educational practices, there will be injustice. There will be those among us who lack compassion and live who unsustainably. My dream is not of Eden, but of a world in which each of us has the capacity to imagine Eden.

I have known many children who cannot imagine living into adulthood, who have never tasted the wind or seen the sunrise, who believe that they are nothing more than their Facebook page or, worse, the numbers they were given in jail and the reports given on the news. While I do not believe my daughter will not fall into this category, I must be aware that I do not raise her in a bubble. Just as I am more than my isolated ego, more than my own parents, she too will be shaped by forces beyond my control. Indeed, for my dream to be possible I must let go of the fear of letting her go. Because of this, my dream is not merely for her, but for the world. The walks she will take with her child will involve an entire Universe, conspiring together: ecological forces that provide the physical context and the cultural forces that allow her to be present to the experience.

In my dream, although there is a whole Universe present in this walk—*because* there is a whole Universe present in this walk—she will, like her father years ago, have no need to check her email during the walk. Her child will be her world. Perhaps this is all I needed to say, perhaps all these words about education have been unnecessary. *Her child will be her world.* If only each child could have such an experience: A little girl, walking on a cool, crisp, sunny autumn day with her father, listening to the leaves blow in the wind and knowing she is enough; a little boy walking with his mother on a shimmering summer day, smelling the flowers and knowing he is enough.

But for my dream to become a reality, for there to be a world in which we care enough to walk with our children, to teach them to be present to and love their world, requires a new paradigm. This is an issue of wisdom. And like all wisdom, it is something that we all possess, but that we must nourish and support in order to express.

My dream for my daughter is not merely that she possesses such wisdom, but that she can grow up in a world and in a culture in which such wisdom is honored and cherished for all, not just for a select few. It can be debated whether such a culture or civilization has existed. Such arguments are pointless, for me. I know it is possible because I can see that possibility in my daughter's eyes. I know it is possible because I can imagine it.

Above all else, to educate must be an act of love. Don't tell me about statistics and outcomes, about the global economy and competing with China. Tell what you love in the world; tell me what you dream for your children. In my dreams, this is how we revolutionize education. My revolution is at once only for my daughter's sake and for the sake of the whole world. A revolution of love.

151

A WISDOM EDUCATION
CURRICULUM
appendix a

The following is a curriculum for a Wisdom Education program. Specifically, this is for a program in an after-school or weekend setting meeting once or twice a week, although it could provide a starting point for a school or classroom curriculum. Because different programs have different schedules, we have provided general themes and areas of focus for each month. Part of the philosophy of Wisdom Education is that both the individual creativity of each student and the collective creativity of each group should express the principles of Wisdom Education—indeed, express their own wisdom—in a unique way. A group in rural New Mexico would obviously have a different expression of this program from a group on the South Side of Chicago.

Implicit in each month is that the Wisdom Education pedagogical approach will be applied. Students should have ample opportunity each month for contemplative practice, creative expression, and experiences in nature even if it is not stated in the curriculum. While the amount of time spent on projects surely increases as the year progresses, students should get time to work on their creativity throughout the year. If few students are ready to begin working on a project, a collaborative project can be initiated—some groups only do a collaborative project that incorporates smaller projects of individual students.

Each month (which can be covered in any amount of time, depending on the schedule and needs of each individual program) has both a theme and a "C" that will be emphasized. There are several categories that are usually covered in each month:

- *Rites of Passage*: Each group should have the opportunity to learn about Rites of Passage. This is usually done in separate boys and girls groups. In some cases, this can be combined with the boys/girls groups.

- *Boys/Girls Circle*: This is an opportunity for the students to discuss what's on their minds and their feelings about the program in a safe space.

- *Creative Response*: Students should have some time to express themselves creatively in class. This can often be in response to some of the material discussed. Particularly early on in the process, it is often helpful to introduce media to the students to expose them to different forms of self-expression.

- *Ancestors*: Wisdom Education is about expanding one's sense of self. One way to do this is to explore our roots. As we understand where we come from, our ideas about who we are expand. This can go beyond our human ancestors.

- *My Community*: Students explore issues of justice in their community and in the world. A particular emphasis is placed on how those issues are connected to each other and to their lives.

- *Cultivating Awareness*: Wisdom Education is not only about what we know, but also about how we experience our world. Too often, our lives are spent staring at screens and not using our senses. The cultivation of awareness is done partly through meditation and partly through activities described below that connect us to the natural world of which we are a part.

- *Trips*: The students' lives can be dramatically enhanced by getting out of the classroom and experiencing natural and cultural activities that get them out of their comfort zone. This is part of the process of expanding their world. We suggest doing this once a month, if possible.

PHASE 1
DISCOVERING OUR PLACE IN THE WORLD

The emphasis of the first phase is how we relate to the world around us, how we define our selves. "Fitting in," of course, does not mean accepting everything that society dictates; rather as we learn how we are in intimate relationship to our world, and learn our true identity, we also learn that we have the capacity to transform our world. Ultimately, the way we define our selves and the world cannot be separated.

September: "Who Am I?"
"C": Character

Introduction
The first class or two should be an opportunity to familiarize the students with the concept of wisdom education. For the most part, the students will have been educated according to the conventional model, so our approach may be foreign to them. They should be given the opportunity to ask questions and to get to know one another.

As important as it is to present some of the philosophy to the students, their participation and enjoyment depends largely on the extent to which they bond with one another. A key concept for the students to explore is community. Through their definition of community, the students should establish some shared expectations for how they should treat one another.

The ideal way to begin is through an outdoor activity or retreat in which the students go through team building activities (such as a ropes course).

Very early in the process, students should learn what Wisdom means, and the difference between wisdom and knowledge. Some ideas about wisdom are as follows:

- Wisdom comes forth from the ability to perceive the whole; knowledge is from a group of isolated facts.
- Wisdom is perceived through the imagination; knowledge is through grasp information intellectually.
- Wisdom is expressed through creativity; knowledge through information.
- Wisdom requires compassion; knowledge is ethically neutral.
- Wisdom and knowledge are not opposites; knowledge is required in order to be wise.

INTRODUCTION TO RITES OF PASSAGE: the Rite of Passage focus for the first month is on helping the group understand what a Rite of Passage is and why it is important. Below is some of the basic information:

What is a Rite of Passage?
- A ceremony, ritual or set of activities that marks the transition from one phase of life to another.
- It may also refer to the process of change an individual goes through while moving from one stage or role in life to another.

Different Types
- Birth- refers to those transitions that signify new beginnings. Example: birth, first day of school, first date, first child, etc.
- Initiation- when one is made a member of a sect or society. Initiation is about learning, being tested, and taking on new responsibilities. Example: coming of age ceremonies, confirmation, bar or bat mitzvah, quinceaneras, etc.
- Partnering- when things come together. Example: engagement, marriage, starting a business partnership, etc.
- Endings- a time of finishing or letting go. Example: death, retirement, divorce, empty nest, etc.

Coming of Age
- Most common form of intentional initiation
- The community helps young people transition from child into adolescence; traditionally the intent is to shift the focus of youth toward their roles in the community.

Initiation
- Initiation is about the creation, maintenance and continuity of the community; it is how cultural knowledge and wisdom is passed on to successive generations.
- Roles are defined and redefined
- It's about finding our home, knowing who we are and where we come from and belonging to a community
- The experience of our elders and ancestors is a part of who we are

PROJECT PROPOSALS: *Discovering my Passion*
While students need not know for certain what their passion is, they should begin the process of figuring out their passion and where their interests lie.

CULTIVATING AWARENESS: *What Does it Mean to be a Human Being?*
This is an exercise about how we define ourselves through the use of metaphor. The following brief exercise will demonstrate this:

Divide the students into three groups. Instruct them that each group will be given a phrase that contains a metaphor about what it means to be a human being. From this phrase they must complete the paragraph.

1) A human being is a child of God. . . .
2) A human being is stardust that has evolved into molecules and organs. . . .
3) A human being is a machine. . . .

Discuss the metaphors. What values do they convey? Which do the students prefer? Why? Which predominate in our society?

157

Creative Response: *"I Am" Poems*
Many students already will be accomplished poets, but others can use some help getting started. The "I am" poem is an easy template for a student to get started. As always, it is fine if the student chooses to deviate from the format. The basic form is seven lines, each starting with "I am." Students can be recorded reading their poem when they finish.

The "I am" poem comes out of a long tradition of sacred texts that use the phrase "I am . . ." as a way to affirm the totality, presence, and vastness of the divine. Often, apparently contradictory statements are found in such poems. For the student, it is a way to begin the process of self-definition.

Ancestors: *My Family*
Students begin the process of exploring their roots by making a family tree

My Community
An issue facing my community/ an issue facing the world (how are these related)

Boys/Girls Circle: *The Roles we Play*
In this exercise, the students explore the different roles they play. Students make a list of the roles they play in their family, at school, and in their community (or "the street"). Students share their lists. Discuss the following paradox:
  a) There is a "Self" that transcends these roles; we are more than the ways in which others define us.
  b) Our "Self" is not isolated from others; in many ways, who we are is defined by our relationships.

October: "Harvest"
"C": Community

Cultivating Awareness: *Where Does My Food Come From?*
The focus on the harvest is a way to (1) cultivate an awareness about the seasonal cycles from which we are often so detached and

(2) expand our sense of who we are and our interconnections to a vast, living world. A simple exercise to do this is to bring a snack and have a contest among the students: who can come up with the most factors that contributed to its getting there. For example, if the snack is a pear, the list might include:

-◆Sunlight
-◆People who picked the fruit
-◆Soil
-◆Oil for transportation
-◆Rain

The list could obviously become quite long as the student begins to consider the web of relationships that allow us to obtain our food.

Trip: *Community Garden/Organic Farm*
It is recommended that programs in urban areas at least get a plot in a community garden, if possible. Around this time of year it would be good for the group to participate in the harvest in some way to get in touch with the process of growing our food. Moreover, learning how to start a community garden could be a great project to improve one's community by encouraging healthy living and reclaiming the commons. A trip to the community garden could provide food for the next activity.

Creative Response: *Preparing a Meal*
Cooking is a creative medium that incorporates all the senses and connects us to our bodies and the natural world around us. The learning possibilities during the process of preparing food are limitless. And of course, the students will love to eat what they prepare. Sharing food is an ancient and beautiful way to build community.

Rites of Passage: *What Does it Mean to be a Man/Woman?*

My Community: *Environmental Racism*
Often, issues of "environmentalism" are considered a concern for the privileged. Instead of "environmentalism," introduce the term

ecology as a way to demonstrate that we are all a part of an ecosystem. In addition, the topic of environmental racism can show the students how this issue affects the marginalized even more than the elite.

Ask the students: "Does the ecological crisis concern you? Why or why not?" Then ask the following questions. See how many students have at least four "yeses."

1) Do you or someone in your family live near a place where there are trucks idling?
2) Do you or someone in your family have asthma?
3) Do you or someone in your family live near a landfill or dump?
4) Are there factories near where you live?
5) Do you know anyone who has suffered from lead poisoning?
6) Do you or does anyone in your family have cancer?
7) Do you live in an area where there are no stores with affordable fruits and vegetables?

Question For Discussion: Would it be as easy to find people to answer "yes" to these questions in a wealthy, white neighborhood? Why?

Ecological Footprint:
- What does the term mean?
- Compare US and another country in Africa (pass out papers)
- Two Students get online and discover theirs by visiting www.myfootprint.org.
- Those students go to www.nationmaster.com/graph/env_eco_foo-environment-ecological-footprint
- Compare large footprints to small ones. What does this have to do with GDP?
- Compared to national average, then to the African country. Why is it different? What does this mean?
- If Americans have to give up a lot of our consumption to save the planet without keeping the rest of the world in poverty, are we willing to do it? Why not?

Boys/Girls Circle: *Dealing with Loss*

November: *"Where do we come from?"*
"C": Cosmology

Rites of Passage: How does a rite of passage relate to our origins? Have the students explore rites of passage from their own cultural or ancestral tradition.

Creation Myths: In understanding where we come from we gain an understanding of who we are. A creation myth is not just an explanation of how the world came to be; it was a way for a culture to define itself and define the relationship of the individual to the whole. Creation myths are an expression of the values of a culture. Students should discuss what a myth is. In the West, we frequently use the term myth to refer to something untrue. The students should explore this further. Although some facts about a myth may not be true, the totality of the wisdom it conveys may be more true than any factual account (WISDOM VS. KNOWLEDGE).

Students should be introduced a one or two creations myths, particularly from traditions that may be in their own cultural heritage. Discuss the stories and the wisdom they conveyed to those people. This is also a good opportunity to introduce the core values of some of the great religious traditions.

What are the myths we live by today? What do they say about our values?

Cosmic Walk: The cosmic walk is an exercise to understand the story of the Universe according to modern science. A 140 foot rope can be used to represent the timeline of the Universe. Numbers should be marked to scale on the rope to indicate each new emergence in the story of the Universe. The rope can be made into a large spiral. Each student chooses a particular number. The following is read and discussed:

The story of the Universe is the story of each of us. Each phase, each moment in this story is the Universe giving birth to us. Each moment represents the birth of our common ancestor. Out of unimaginable light the universe was dreamed into being. It contained all the light, energy, and potential for everything that would ever come to be, all contained within the vessel of hydrogen.

(1) *The Primordial Fireball (13.7 Billion years ago)*

(2) *Stars (13.3 Billion years ago)*

(3) *Galaxies (12.7 Billion years ago)*

(4) *Expansion (7 Billion years ago) Dark energy overpowers the gravitational pull of Dark Matter and the expansion of the universe accelerates.*

(5) *Supernova (4.6 billion years ago) Our mother star, in the Orion arm of the Milky Way galaxy, having consumed and sacrificed herself, collapsed. In the intense energy of that collapse, she was transformed into a supernova, exploding her stardust into space, and birthing all the new elements which would take shape as Earth's body and ours.*

(6) *Sun (4.5 billion years ago) That exploding stardust began to slow down, cool, and condense into a community of planets around the mother star, our Sun.*

(7) *Earth (4.1 billion years ago) Our planet slowly cooled and gradually formed an atmosphere, oceans, and land mass.*

(8) *Life (4 billion years ago) Gradually, within the oceans, more complex arrangements began to take shape. These were the first simple cells, and through them, Earth awakened into life.*

(9) *Photosynthesis (3.9 billion years ago) Earth learned to take nourishment from the Sun. Through these simple-celled microbes, she learned to eat sunlight, to nurse from the Sun. And that dynamic laid the pattern for all future life forms, that each must receive nourishment from another, and give itself in return to become nourishment for another.*

(10) *Sexual reproduction (1 billion years ago) life was mysteriously drawn toward union, and the first simple-celled organisms began to reproduce sexually. Different strands of genetic memory were combined in the new offspring. This opened up infinite new possibilities. Around the same time, organisms began to feed on other organisms, and that relationship formed the basis of the community in which each would develop.*

(11) *Birds (150 million years ago) the first birds took flight, and in and through them Earth broke into melody and song.*

(12) *Flowers (120 million years ago) The first flowering plants emerged, concentrating their life energy and memory into seed, making protein in the form of seed available for the mammals who were yet to come, and, in their flowering, bringing color and fragrance to Earth.*

(13) *Mammals (114 million years ago) The first placental mammals developed, warm-blooded creatures who, like the supernova, carry their unborn young within their own bodies, and who nourish them from their own substance both before and after their birth.*

(14) *Earliest Hominids (2.6 million years ago) The earliest hominid types evolved from the primate mammals in Africa. Creatures with brains and nervous systems complex enough that in and through them Earth awakened into self- conscious awareness of her existence.*

(15) *"Eve" (70,000 years ago) Our common ancestor, our great grandmother, "mitochondrial Eve" lived in Africa. There were only two thousand human beings at this time. Soon after, some of these humans began to leave Africa to populate the rest of the Earth.*

Today, in this moment of grace, all humans can finally understand their common origin story, embracing and celebrating their different stories within a single Earth community in a single sacred universe. Like the Uroboros, the beginning of the Universe is like the end: each of us, right now, carries with us the memories of this story. Within us, we have the capacity to give birth to a new world.

There are many discussion points from this exercise. How do the students feel about the scientific account of the Universe? Is it overwhelming? Does it feel meaningless? Do they prefer it to the religious accounts they may have heard? The task of the facilitator is not to tell the students what to believe; rather, the teacher should ask the students to accept the story for now and consider what it might mean for how we treat one another. What if each moment in this story represented the story of our own becoming? What if this were the story of our ancestors and us? What if we were all related? How does this story relate to other creation myths?

Finally, have the students make a timeline of their own lives, past, present, and future, marking the points of emergence (rites of passage) in their own lives.

Creative Response: *Creating a Mandala*

A mandala is a visual representation of the Universe (Macrocosm) and the Individual (Microcosm). Using a pencil-compass, protractor, and colored pencils, students can create their own.

- First, have the students make concentric circles.
- Second, have them divide the circles into eight equal slices.
- The students should then create patterns within each section. Around each circle, the patterns should be repeating.
- Students color the mandala.
- Finally, in the center, the students create a symbol that represents their true selves.

Ancestors: *Exploring our Roots*

The students can now go beyond the family tree to explore their deeper roots—that is the culture to which they trace their ancestry beyond their known ancestors. If possible, students could do a DNA test to determine this, or use ancestry.com.

Trip: *Telescope Viewing / Planetarium*

If students live in a big city with a lot of light pollution, they could go to a planetarium; otherwise, they could use a telescope to look at the stars. This makes a good follow-up to the Cosmic Walk—students should understand that as they look deep into space, they are looking into the past. For many students, simply going out at night in a rural setting can be awe inspiring.

Boys / Girls Circle: *Exploring Feelings About our Families*

December: *"Our Values"*
"C": *Compassion*

Rites of Passage: Begin to explore some rites of passage from other cultures. This is an opportunity to continue the discussion about some of humanity's great religious traditions.

My Community: *GDP*
Students explore the values of our culture by studying the GDP. Some may have heard of it and may know what it stands for, but few will understand what it means for our communities. For most politicians, a growing economy and GDP is the highest value. But the GDP grows for *any* economic activity. Make a list of some things that may not be so positive but grow the GDP:

- Someone gets cancer
- An oil spill
- Someone gets arrested
- A prison is built
- We declare war

Explore one or two of these that directly have affected the students' community. What does this day about our values as a society? What is the difference between equating life or existence with value and the dollar? What are the students' values?

Cultivating Awareness: *Plants/Brand Names*
Split students into two groups. Ask each group to make a list of as many brand names as they can come up with in five minutes. Then do the same with species of plants. Usually, the list of brands is much longer. Why? What does this say about what we focus on in our lives? What has more value, a plant or a brand name?

Creative Response: *Making a Movie*
Students can start learning to make a movie by filming class or recitations of poems or raps. iMovie is an easy way to edit footage to begin the process of creating a film.

Economics/ecology
Perhaps no subject could demonstrate the values of our society than economics. We have made economics primary, when it in fact

describes a subset of ecology. Both come from the Greek word *oikos*, meaning home. Ecology refers to the web of relationships that support life—including us. Our primary home is the ecosystem of which we are a part. Economics originally referred to the way we manage the resources of our home. It now refers to the way the human manages the resources of the planet. Money, an abstraction of these resources, is the primary way to ascribe value to these resources in economics. How does this fail to account for the true value of life?

Boys/Girls Circle: What are your values? What are society's values? How are they different?

PHASE 2
REIMAGINING OUR WORLD

While the focus of the first phase was on how we define our selves, finding our place in the universe, and our relationship to the world around us, the second phase emphasizes our ability to transform the world through our creativity. In many ways, the world we inhabit as human beings is defined by the stories we tell. Phase 2 emphasizes our empowering students to transform our world in ways that contrast the mainstream culture.

The students' creative work is now directed toward the creative projects, if it has not already been. Each student should now be paired with mentors at this point. This can be individually or a single mentor for a few students working together.

January: "Media Awareness"
"C": Critical Consciousness

Projects: *Turning the Passion into a Project*
If the students have not already begun their projects, they should take a few classes to identify what they are doing. By this time, it is helpful if the students have mentors to help with this process.

Rites of Passage: *Beginning to Create our Own Ceremony*
While there are certain elements of the Rite of Passage that will
be given to the students, the students can and should have input
about certain elements of the ceremony. By now, they snould have
a pretty good understanding of what a traditional ceremony looks
like. From the template given and an exploration of some traditional ceremonies, the students can offer ideas about what their rite
of passage can look like.

Dr. Martin Luther King, Jr.: *"Creatively Maladjusted"*
Students often hear a great deal about Dr. King around his holi-
day. Unfortunately, much of it is watered down. Students hear a lot
about the "I have a dream" speech, and King's emphasis on non-
violence. These are noble ideas, but seldom do they learn that king
opposed American imperialism and capitalism just as he opposed
segregation. Clearly his dream has not yet been realized. This lesson centers on this quote: "Human salvation lies in the hands of the
creatively maladjusted." That is, there is nothing wrong with those
of us who are "maladjusted." We should be. Our task is to make
our maladjustment creative, not destructive.

Media Awareness Curriculum
Media Awareness is increasingly important in cultural environment
saturated with media. Our students often spend almost all of their
time plugged into something or in front of a screen. While we hope
to get them to turn it off sometimes, we must be aware that our
youth still must learn to navigate through much more information
than most of us did as kids. The Chicago Wisdom Project has used
the *Adbusters Media Empowerment Kit*. For more information, see
the websites in the back of this manual. If you choose to create your
media awareness classes, consider the following:

 ↬Encourage the students to consider how much time they
  spend in an electronic environment
 ↬Look at some commercials together. What techniques are being used to convince us to buy a particular product?

~&Observe some music videos. Examine the images of women, African-Americans and others. Where do these notions come from?

~&What is the underlying message of some of the television programs the students watch, particularly "reality" programs.

~&Research the major news outlets. Who owns them? How might this affect what they report?

~&Discuss several recent events in the news. Has this discussion changed the way you might view the way those events were reported? What biases do you think might have occurred and why?

Boys/Girls Circle: By this time, the discussions in these groups can be largely determined by issues that come up among the students.

February: "Meditation and Martial Arts"
"C": Contemplation

In this month the emphasis is on the experience and practice of martial arts and meditation. If there is no experienced martial arts teacher on staff, one should be found from elsewhere.

Warrior vs. Soldier
As a discussion point, ask the students to explain the differences and similarities between a soldier and a warrior. The idea is that, as our students enter into manhood and womanhood, they will become warriors.

~&Both warriors and soldiers must show courage to fight

~&A warrior fights peacefully; a soldier only fights violently

~&A warrior only uses violence when all other possibilities have been exhausted; a soldier fights because he is told to fight

~&A warrior thinks for himself; a soldier follows orders

~&A warrior fights external battles (for justice) and internal ones (in the soul); a soldier can only fight others

~&The warrior learns to heal the past and not be afraid of the future, thus live in the now

Rites of Passage: *Solitude*

The emphasis for this month is solitude, an important element of the rite of passage experience. Have the students meditate by themselves for a few minutes, then reflect in their journals about the experience: Where did your mind go when there was silence? How often do you have solitude—without music, TV, etc.? Why is it difficult to be alone? Discuss

March: Chaos

Introduction to Chaos
- What does chaos mean?
- Why should we study chaos?
- How has chaos come up in my own life?
- What happens when people are afraid of chaos, try to crush chaos by controlling everything?

Students are to write about a way that chaos has come up in their lives. Keep what the students have written as they will be referred to at the end of the unit to see what has changed.

Chaos in the Universe Story: We will refer back to the Cosmic Walk from earlier in the year to discuss the role of chaos in creation.
- Chaos in the primordial fireball
- Chaos in the Supernovas
- Chaos in the evolutionary process on planet Earth

Chaos in Mythology: Again referring back to the cosmology unit, we explore the role of chaos in mythology. What do our religious traditions say about chaos?
- Chaos in Creation Myths: For example, Chaos and Cosmos (Greek)
- The Trickster: For example, Elegba (from the Yoruba tradition); Coyote

My Ancestors: *Chaos in History*

169

- The Middle Passage
- Examples of historical figures who dealt with chaos and transformed it into something positive (e.g. Malcolm X)

Creative Response: *The Role of Chaos in Art*
- Who are some characters from books or movies who have dealt with chaos and transformed it into something positive? (e.g. *The Color Purple*)
- We have already looked at the Middle Passage and slavery as an example of chaos in history. What were some of the creative forms that emerged from this experience? Jazz, blues . . . others?
- *Hip Hop*: Hip Hop emerged in the 1970s in the South Bronx, an area that had been devastated by drugs and violence.
- *Improv Theater*: how does the controlled chaos of improv make it more interesting, funnier, more creative?

How can our art bring order out of the chaos of our lives? Encourage the students to integrate a chaotic element into their creative projects.

My Community: *Chaos in the World Today*
- Katrina
- Global Warming
- Violence

Rites of Passage: Discuss the element of chaos in a rite of passage ceremony. Instead of avoiding chaos or pretending it's not there, a rite of passage experience encourages us to confront chaos to return to order.

Boys/Girls Group
Students write about and discuss chaos in their lives:
- One example of chaos that they hope to bring to order

⤳One example of chaos that they are grateful for.

The students can refer back to what the students wrote in the first chaos lesson. Has their view of chaos changed?

April: *"Our Food, Our Bodies"*
"C": Courage

Community Garden Project
Depending on the climate in which this program takes place, this may be the ideal month in which to start a community garden project. Such a project is an ideal way to apply some of the ideas learned earlier in the year:
⤳Students must take a leadership role in their community. They will have to contact people in order to get permission, and recruit members of their community to join.
⤳The students will have to research gardening.
⤳The students must become acquainted with their bioregion, the specific place in which they live.

My Community: *What we Eat*
This lesson explores the issue of the lack of healthy food in certain neighborhoods and ways that the mass media promotes unhealthy food in marginalized communities. The students then explore the food industry at large. How and why is food distributed around the world. How does this affect us? How is this unjust? Students should keep a "food diary"—a list of everything they eat—for a week before this class.

Boys/Girls Circle: *A Discussion About Body Image*

Rites of passage: What is the role of food in a ceremony or celebration? What food should we have for ours that best reflects the spirit of this process? The students can and should make decisions about

171

this, but should understand what is appropriate. Discuss food for the celebration that is:

- ⟶ Local (from their garden, if possible)
- ⟶ Healthy
- ⟶ Connected to their cultural tradition

PHASE 3
PREPARING FOR TRANSFORMATION

As the Rite of Passage approaches, special attention is now paid to the gravity of that experience. It is important that students are emotional, physically, intellectually, and spiritually prepared for the experience.

May: Creativity

As the students approach the end of the year, classroom time can be almost completely devoted to finishing projects. In addition, some time should be set aside for reflection on the process in the boys and girls circles.

In addition, plenty of time should be given to preparing for the rite of passage.

PHASE 4
TRANSFORMING MY SELF

The final phase of the program comes after the normal class time has ended. This includes the presentation of the projects, the retreat, and the rite of passage ceremony.

Summer Months: "Ceremony, Celebration, & Ritual"

Retreat: The retreat is an important part of the Wisdom Education experience. While the specifics of the retreat will vary from program to program, some elements to include are:

- ⟶ The retreat should occur away from the city so the students can be in tune with nature.

- ◆There should be a balance between organized activities and the opportunity for the students to reflect quietly.
- ◆Students should have the opportunity to reflect on and process the entire experience in Boys/Girls Groups.
- ◆Students should feel safe, but also get out of their comfort zone to some degree.

Rite of Passage: The culmination of the retreat is the rite of passage ceremony. At this point, the students leave behind certain elements of their previous selves and enter into a new way of relating to their world and themselves.

Presentation of Creative Projects: The students present their projects to the community. During this experience, they should stand up before their peers, their families, and others and speak confidently about what they have done. The community should be encouraged to ask difficult questions.

THE TEN Cs[1]

appendix b

(1) Contemplation (p.108): All lessons should begin with meditation or with specific healing art practice of the class. Students should understand the basic meaning and purpose of contemplation and meditation, as well as the philosophy and cosmology underpinning the practice.

(2) Character and Chakra Development (p.138): In order to see the interconnectedness, the contemplative practice can move right into a discussion of Character. Contemplative practice serves not only to find inner peace, but also to cultivate one's character in facing the world. What are the attributes that make up a person's character?

(3) Cosmology & Ecology (p.104): The human body, as discussed in the first two Cs, is not separate from the world, but part of an interconnected community of beings. While both cosmology and ecology will be studied extensively, students should understand some basic definitions:

[1] From Matthew Fox, The A.W.E. Project: Reinventing Education, Reinventing the Human

175

- ☙Ecology comes from the Greek "*Oikos*" meaning "home." It refers to the living community that is our true home.
- ☙Cosmology comes from the Greek "*Cosmos*" meaning both "beauty" and "order." It refers to the study of the Universe and how we can find a meaningful and unique place in it. Cosmology is how we see our connections to one another and the world.

(4) Chaos & Darkness (p.115): Chaos provides the balance for Cosmos. Students should recognize the difference between opposites (e.g. good and evil) and the dynamic tension of concepts like chaos and cosmos (or yin and yang, which is particularly important if students are using a contemplative practice based on the Chinese system). It refers to "disorder" now, but comes from a Greek word meaning "void" or emptiness. At this point, students should become familiar with both of these definitions. To begin with, ask the students what associations they make with chaos and darkness. If students come up with negative associations, encourage them to begin to think of how they can be seen positively.

(5) Compassion (p.121): Students should understand the meaning of compassion. It literally means "to feel with" (Latin *com*=with/*pathos*=feel). This is different from feeling sorry for someone or even to do what one thinks is fair. An emphasis can be placed how compassion is linked with a mother's care for a child. Students will be encouraged to see how they can live their lives more compassionately.

(6) Community (p.130): In many ways, one's capacity for compassion has to do with how community is defined. The students should define what their community is. Students also should be encouraged to think of community in ways that move beyond physical proximity.

(7) Critical Consciousness & Judgment (p.126): What does it mean

176

to think critically? When we are given information, do we always accept it? Whom do we trust? Friends? Parents? Peers?

(8) Courage: *"Compassion is not possible if we lack courage"* (p.124). And our Critical Consciousness doesn't do us much good without courage, either. Ask the students for examples of courageous people.

(9) Creativity (p.111): Students should recognize how the pedagogy is different in its emphasis on the student's creativity. Instead of being given information to learn, the students become teachers as they integrate lessons and experiences and express them in their own, unique way.

(10) Ceremony, Celebration, & Ritual (p.136): Questions for discussion:

- What rituals do you have in your lives?
- Why is ritual important for people of every culture and how does it build community? What rituals do you have in your lives?
- What happens to a society that has lost its rituals? An example: gang initiations that have arisen in the absence of traditional rites of passage.

THE FIVE PILLARS OF
THE CHICAGO WISDOM PROJECT
appendix c

(1) Wisdom of the Elders: C.W.P. differs from many creative arts programs in that we provide guidance to ensure that the creative process makes the student's life more meaningful and encourages a more just, compassi<nate, and sustainable world.

(2) Creativity: Instead of starting with tests and facts that make learning seem boring, C.W.P. begins with the student's passion. It is through the creative expression of this passion that a vision of a more sustainable and just world is possible because it is through our collective creative efforts that we create a worldview.

(3) Connection to Nature: Our alienation from the natural processes of which we are a part is one of the great tragedies of modern life. Many students spend no time in nature and experience themselves as completely cut off from the natural world. Rediscovering this connection to nature can enrich each person's life and foster new insights and creative responses.

(4) Mentoring: This is an educational model that allows us to focus

on the individual interests and passions of the student, rather than attempting to fit all students into the same box. Students will also have the opportunity to become mentors themselves, learning the responsibility of teaching their peers.

(5) Rites of Passage: This is an opportunity for a young person to reconnect to her or his community and the broader world, a way to connect to one's ancestors who experienced similar rites of passage in various forms, and a transformative experience of entering into adulthood.

"OUTCOMES"
appendix d

While we consider this work to be an organic process, one that cannot be reduced to specific outcomes, one that is different each time and for each student, and one that is full of surprises, we hope that we can say the following about our students:

- ❧Students should complete a creative project, giving them a sense of their ability to accomplish something meaningful.
- ❧Students should expand their sense of who they are by seeing themselves as part of a broader community and as having deeper connections to their ancestors.
- ❧Students should begin to see the future in terms of possibilities rather than limitations.
- ❧Students should have the confidence, after completing their rite of passage and their project, to teach others.
- ❧Students should have a sense of their passion, that which gives them a sense of meaning in life.
- ❧Students should be aware of the issues that face their community and other communities around the world and how those issues are interconnected.
- ❧Students should have a greater appreciation for nature.

RESOURCES AND NETWORKING IN THE WISDOM EDUCATION MOVEMENT

appendix e

Wisdom Education does not have a corporate, hierarchical structure like most institutions in the industrial, Western world. Instead, there is a web of interconnected organizations, each with the freedom to express its wisdom in its own way. In this manner, we are all working together to form a movement to radically transform education. This is a fluid and growing list. Below are some contacts for the Wisdom Education movement:

> Y.E.L.L.A.W.E. Project
> C/O Friends of Creation Spirituality
> Oakland, California
> 510-835-0655
> www.matthewfox.org
> 33dennis@sbcglobal.net

> The Chicago Wisdom Project
> 5655 S. University Ave
> Chicago, IL 60637
> 646-285-8263
> info@chicagowisdomproject.org

WEBSITES

Y.E.L.L.A.W.E. · yellawe.org
The Chicago Wisdom Project · chicagowisdomproject.org
Rite of Passage Journeys · riteofpassagejourneys.org
Animas Valley Institute (Rites of Passage) · animas.org
Adbusters · adbusters.org
Ancestry and Genealogy · ancestry.com
Ecological Impacts · myfootprint.org

Chicago Wisdom Project Partners
Sue Duncan Children's Center · sueduncanchildrenscenter.org
University Church · universitychurchchicago.org
YOUTHBUILD · youthbuild.org
Mosaic Multicultural Foundation · mosaicvoices.org

Y.E.L.L.A.W.E. partners
Attitudinal Healing Connection · ahc-oakland.org
Academy for the Love of Learning (ALL) · aloveoflearning.org

BOOKS

William Ayers, *Teaching Toward Freedom: Moral Commitment and Ethical Action in the Classroom*

Jeffrey M. Duncan-Andrade, Ernest Morrell, *The Art of Critical Pedagogy: Possibilities*

Kevin K. Kumashiro, *The Seduction of Common Sense: How the Right has Framed the Debate on America's Schools (Teaching for Social Justice)*

Matthew Fox, *The A.W.E. Project: Reinventing Education, Reinventing the Human*

Paulo Freire, *Pedagogy of the Oppressed*

Richard Louv, *Last Child in the Woods: Saving our Children from Nature-Deficit Disorder*

Kokomon Clottey, *Mindful Drumming: Ancient Wisdom for Unleashing the Human Spirit and Building Community*

Theodore Richards, *Cosmosophia: Cosmology, Mysticism, and the Birth of a New Myth*

R. Sambuli Mosha, *The Heartbeat of Indigenous Africa: A Study of the Chagga Educational System*

Lucia Chiavola Birnbaum, *Dark Mother: African Origins and Godmothers*

Neil Postman, *The End of Education: Redefining the Value of School*

Sir Ken Robinson: *Out of Our Minds: Learning to be Creative*

Bill Plotkin, *Soulcraft*

Walter Feinberg, *Understanding Education: Toward a Reconstruction of Educational Inquiry*

Malidoma Some, *Of Water and Spirit*

Brian Swimme and Thomas Berry, *The Universe Story*

M.C. Richards, *Centering in Pottery. Poetry, and the Person*

John Dewey, *Experience and Education*

BIBLIOGRAPHY

Ato, John. *Dictionary of Word Origins.* New York: Arcade, 1990.

Ayers, William. *Teaching Toward Freedom: Moral Commitment and Ethical Action in the Classroom.* Boston: Beacon Press, 2004.

Beilock, Sian. *Choke: What the Secrets of the Brain Reveal about Getting it Right When you Have To.* New York: Simon & Schuster, 2010.

Berry, Thomas. *The Dream of the Earth.* Sierra Club Books, 2006.

Berry, Thomas and Swimme, Brian. *The Universe Story: From the Primordial Flaring Forth to the Ecozoic Era—A Celebration of the Unfolding Cosmos.* New York: Harper Collins, 1994.

Berry, Wendell. *Bringing it to the Table: On Farming and Food.* Berkeley: Counterpoint, 2009.

Birnbaum, Lucia Chiavola. *Dark Mother: African Origins and Godmothers.*

Clottey, Kokomon. *Mindful Drumming: Ancient Wisdom for Unleashing the Human Spirit and Building Community.* Oakland: Sankofa, 2003.

Dewey, John. *Experience and Education.* New York: Touchstone, 1997.

187

Duncan-Andrade, Jeffrey M.R and Morrell, Ernest. *The Art of Critical Pedagogy: Possibilities for Moving from Theory to Practice in Urban Schools.* New York: Peter Lang, 2008.

Feinberg, Walter. *Understanding Education: Toward a Reconstruction of Educational Inquiry.* New York: Cambridge University Press, 1983.

Fox, Matthew *The A.W.E. Project, Reinventing Education, Reinventing the Human.* Westminster John Knox Press, 2006.

Freire, Paulo. *Pedagogy of the Oppressed.* New York, Penguin, 1993.

Gardner, Howard. *Multiple Intelligences: New Horizons in Theory and Practice.* New York: Basic Books, 1993.

Gramsci, Antonio. *Selections from Prison Notebooks.* London: New Left Books, 1971.

Kumashiro, Kevin K. *The Seduction of Common Sense: How the Right Has Framed the Debate on America's Schools.* New York: Teacher's College Press, 2008.

Lakoff, George. *The Political Mind: A Cognitive Scientist's Guide to your Brain and its Politics* (New York: Penguin, 2009)
_____, *Don't Think of an Elephant: Know Your Values and Frame the Debate.* New York: Chelsea Green, 2004.

Louv, Richard. *The Last Child in the Woods: Saving our Children from Nature-Deficit Disorder.* Chapel Hill: Algonquin Books, 2008.

Mosha, R. Sambuli. *The Heartbeat of Indigenous Africa: A Study of the Chagga Educational System.* New York: Routledge, 2000.

Ong, Walter J. *Orality and Literacy.* New York: Taylor & Francis, 2002.

Postman, Neil. *The End of Education: Redefining the Value of School* (New York: Knopf, 1996.

Plotkin, Bill. *Soulcraft: Crossing into the Mysteries of Nature and Pscyhe.* Novato, CA: New World Library, 2003.

Ray, Paul and Anderson, Sherry. *Cultural Creatives: How Fifty Million People are Changing the World.* New York: Harmony Books, 2000.

Richards, M.C. *Centering in Poetry and Pottery.* Wesleyan University Press, 1989.

Richards, Theodore. *Cosmosophia: Cosmology, Mysticism, and the Birth of a New Myth*. Hiraeth Press, 2011.

Robinson, Ken. *Out of our Minds: Learning to be Creative*. New York: Wiley, John & Sons, 2001.

Roszak, Theodore. *The Cult of Information: The Folklore of Computers and the True Art of Thinking*. New York: Pantheon.

Some, Malidoma Patrice. *Of Water and the Spirit: Ritual, Magic, and Initiation in the Life of an African Shaman*. New York: Penguin, 1994.

ACKNOWLEDGMENTS

Thank you:

To Hiraeth Press: My editor and friend, L.M. Browning, and Jason Kirkey.

To my teachers: There are too many to name and some will surely be forgotten, but I would like to make a special reference to Sue, Tony and the many wonderful teachers at CIIS.

To all the kids at the Sue Duncan Children's Center in Chicago, to the Y.E.L.L.A.W.E. kids in Oakland, and to all the Chicago Wisdom Project students, past and present.

To Bill Ayers, Matthew Fox, James Speights, and Julian DeShazier for your kind readings and comments on my manuscript.

To everyone who has helped out at the Chicago Wisdom Project: Natacha Walker, Carmen Bowman, Mike Kristovic, Mollie Dowling, Owen Duncan, Ryan Hollon, Paul Sakol, Angela Charlton, Matthew Relstab, Kasabez Maakmaah, Danny Gordon, Meg Peterson, Kedest Kassahun, Cullen Barry, Gene Smitherman, Diane Wolverton, Zuberri Badili, Dan Nuemann, Tomas Ramirez, Louie Bedar, Charles Fitzpatrick, Mike & Brian Moran, and Rachel Faulkner.

To my family, who taught me the value of education.

And to my daughter, Cosima, and my wife, Arianne, for everything.

ABOUT THE AUTHOR

Theodore Richards, PhD, is a poet, writer, and religious philosopher. He is the author of numerous articles and poems and of *Handprints on the Womb*, a collection of poetry; *Cosmosophia: Cosmology, Mysticism, and the Birth of a New Myth*, recipient of the Independent Publisher Awards Gold Medal in religion; and the novel *The Crucifixion*. Richards is the founder and executive director of The Chicago Wisdom Project and a dean and lecturer on world religions at The New Seminary. He lives in Chicago with his wife and daughter. For more information on Theodore and his work, please visit www.theodorerichards.com and www.chicagowisdomproject.org.